ADULTERER

ADULTERER

A Story of Infidelity and Faith

W. J. M. MARTIN

RESOURCE *Publications* • Eugene, Oregon

ADULTERER
A Story of Infidelity and Faith

Resource Publications
An Imprint of Wipf and Stock Publishers
199 W. 8th Ave., Suite 3
Eugene, OR 97401

www.wipfandstock.com

PAPERBACK ISBN: 978-1-6667-1646-7
HARDCOVER ISBN: 978-1-6667-1647-4
EBOOK ISBN: 978-1-6667-1648-1

NOVEMBER 2, 2021 10:53 AM

But those who commit adultery have no sense;

those who do it destroy themselves.

PROVERBS 6:32

CONTENTS

A Marriage Blessing | ix

I   The Push | 1

II   The Liar | 6

III   God Speaks | 11

IV   Satan Speaks | 18

V   Two Sides | 24

VI   Love | 29

VII   Sacred Lesson | 36

VIII   A Point of View | 42

IX   The Face of Darkness | 49

X   Symbolum | 57

XI   First Confession | 65

XII   The Refuge of Sinners | 76

XIII   Second Confession | 84

A MARRIAGE BLESSING

Heavenly Father, through the intercession of the Holy Family,
Help us treasure the gift of marriage that reflects the love of
Christ for the Church,
where the self-giving love of husband and wife
unites them more perfectly
and cooperates in your plan for new life created in your image.
Amen.

I

THE PUSH

No one comes into this world with an innate desire to break the seventh commandment. I certainly didn't. Baptism welcomed me into a family that God had justly ordained for my earthy sojourn. Tragically original sin had already commenced eroding its domestic foundation before I even arrived.

I am a Catholic, born into the faith during a time of great ecclesiastical stability. I was taught the faith in a time of great doctrinal instability. I finally abandoned my faith at a time of great personal volatility.

My earthly father was a serial philanderer, unhappy in his life choices and retreating to women and drink. Subsequently I spent most of my teenaged years believing that being raised in that sinful environment instilled a visceral disgust for that type of behavior. It was logical to assume that watching a dishonest person destroy their own life would naturally spawn me into living an honest life. My early willful rejection of my father's lack of morality gave me a sense of moral awareness that I took great pride in. It separated me from his world of sin and elevated my disgust for him almost to the point of hating him. I surely felt justified in my judgements.

When I finally married I resolved to be the most loyal of husbands and turn the page in one complete and final rejection of my father's legacy. To stay loyal and true to my spouse to the end.

And I did.

For 10 years I persevered in my quest for total marital fidelity. To be a good husband and father came natural to me as if I was blessed with a domestic fortitude that had escaped my own dad. I flourished in my individual way, finding a love and strength I had never known to be possible.

Traits that certainly were never taught to me by my parents. It was period of great revelation. I learned that I was capable of being the type of superior care giver and marital partner that I once feared I never could be.

So it was that truth and belief which ruled my world and the knowledge that God held my family within the palm of his hand and that the true model of the Holy Family was the architype for the whole of mankind. That nothing in the universe meant more to its creator than the embodiment of this model for his own earthly creations. I was living the scripture, the holy life and a model of *the* model.

Then something happened that seemed be an impossibly, an absurdity. God abandoned me.

His hand had opened. My family came tumbling out. The pattern of all that was deemed perfect was smashed. Life started to unravel. Issues from the past now harshly exposed the inherent flaws in my marriage and suddenly it ended in chaos and confusion. Pain and suffering ensued with all the expected breakup complications; children going back and forth, financial concerns, property liquidation, the works. Angers flared with blame and who to blame becoming the daily conversations. Ultimately, eventually I laid much of that blame on the one in whom I placed all my trust.

Our Father, my loving protector, my God, my betrayer.

How could he allow this? What sort of lies was I led to believe? The Holy Family, pattern for the world? Saint John Paul II wrote a whole Apostolic Exhortation, *Familiaris Consortio*, on how it should all play out. Every detail, every ideal. It was the

Popes impression of the God's blueprint for the human family, the family of God. And we followed it. We followed all the rubrics, the sacraments, the routines. We went to church, said grace at every meal, got involved with our parish. Followed all the do's and don'ts. But obviously it wasn't enough for the almighty one. We didn't tick off enough 'must do's' on God's immense check list. And so the almighty withdrew from my family in His disgust.

My family crumbled. My wife left, struggling with this demon and that ghost. Children being children remained bewildered and confused. And I became angry . . . very angry, for many years to follow.

Drifting in and out a spiritual awakening and re-awakening and re-re awakening became the trend. Well-meaning acquaintances would bring advice and explain the subtle differences behind Gods 'actual' plan and man's fallen version of it, but the story always had the same ending and the same result. Me without my family.

Life settled into a rhythm of belief and possible belief and un-belief and back again. At times my faith was strong, to the point of joining a tertiary religious order, then weak, to the point of not attending church for a full year. Working considerably and scrambling between my children's functions kept me busy enough. Women or more correctly the need for a woman was masked behind all the external factors that come along with being a recently made single parent with two kids.

Of course sooner or later, the male urges would return. And they did. And when they did my eyes began to roam about, hungry and curious. Eventually they settled on a fellow worker. The classic situation. Textbook. The work place relationship which, as we know, has been studied, reviewed, novelized and scandalized to death.

It always starts off innocently, or under the appearance of an innocent action, as in going for a walk in the park. A lunch time stroll, just a stretch of the legs as it was described in a famous movie. Two fellow workers taking advantage of the beautiful gardens in close proximity to our office. Healthy activity, which became a pretty good stratagem. In reality the invitation was a scam from the very first suggestion. I knew she liked the idea before I even proposed it. She was vulnerable and I was eager. There was only one problem, one major problem, she was married. I was in lust and all I really wanted was fornication. I hadn't really intended to break multiple commandments simultaneously.

But she was married. And not happily, in fact the total opposite. It was a long miserable marriage. But this really isn't about her susceptibility. This is about my journey from darkness to light, then back and forth and back again. It was an endless dance with reason and the supernatural. Did God really care one way or another? He abandoned me to my own devices and now I was left with the decisions I had to make. I knew what I wanted. I wanted her. Thus was the beginning of a long conflict with lust, love, fear and the spiritual world. Both sides would fight for my soul, like a great Civil War conflict, the battlefield front being pushing one way and then back again by two powerful opposing armies. And even as it raged I knew that one day the battle would cease but with the outcome wholly uncertain.

There were times when I could clearly see my error and my actions seemed completely in opposition to who I really was deep inside, but it never stopped me.

Secret plans were drawn up and rendezvous where to be had. We went off, to and fro and did the things adults do under the cloak of desire and we enjoyed every single minute of it.

The risk and danger meant nothing. All that mattered was plunging deeper into the abyss. Never would I anticipate the ferocity with which the evil enemy would fight off any chance that I would give up on my self-destruction even to the point of having to reveal himself. Only in a supreme act of desperation will the Devil actually allow himself to be seen pulling your strings. He's a whisperer, a suggestor. The less you know about his reality the better. But I saw him in action. I felt him. The Devil was real and not a mythical creation conjured up in ancient and obscure Middle Eastern texts. Evil would ultimately manifest itself to me. The truth of its existence would be made physical in total opposition to the modern view of the supernatural being nothing more than fantasy and superstition.

And yet it is an odd thing, to be afraid of the certainty of the devil and his schemes but to dismiss the certainty of God out of anger and lust. That's the beauty of mankinds' weakness. We can be easily played.

And when you want to break one or two of His commandments, anger is a great excuse. Deny the commandments, dismiss the concepts. Since God was not 'I AM', then I was not either.

I chose to go the very widest path.

✳

Happiness is something we all certainly hope to achieve. Most of us experience happiness during different periods throughout our lives, at least to some extent. It comes and goes. Losing my wife started a period of great unhappiness. Finding my lover began a period of measurable happiness which came in changeable degrees. She filled a hole in my heart and a hole in my ego. She listened to me, laughed at my jokes. She confided in me, told me things, deep things, as well as sharing a true friendship with me. And of course, she also took care of my sexual needs. There is no doubt that without the sex, all the other parts of the equation would be far less than the whole. At least at the beginning. You can lie to yourself about many things but desire and human functionality are not one of those things. A person can disguise it, try to master it or generally try to ignore it, but it is always there. The hunger, the need. Not even age totally defeats it, only death. I wanted her and that was all there was to it. And neither Hell nor the threat thereof was going to stop me. In fact Hell would be assisting me

II

THE LIAR

Twisting and turning like snakes we slid through the affair. Parked cars, hotel rooms, wooded seclusions, strange and stranger settings all adding fuel to the pyre. It almost became normal and natural, expected. In a crazy way we thought of ourselves as a real couple, at least to help cover our own deceitfulness. It wasn't hard to find new ways to be convinced of the righteous purpose behind our fling. Her husband was a bum. A real and true bum. Not my imagination and not a constructed excuse. He was a bum. The type of man most other men loathed to be around and that all women feared.

A bad father, a bad husband, a bad citizen, a bad drunkard, a bad man. A dangerous, angry, petty, abusive, disdainful, rotten to the core bastard. So playing our game wasn't really playing a game but more saving a ruined woman from the clutches of an ogre. I was a white knight, all clean and justified, shimmering under the mantle of my good deeds. Grand and exceptional I was, all while getting as much sex as I could handle in compensation.

The journey from good guy to liar began with the breakup of my marriage. It felt like an eternity in my past from once being a man of honor and of his word, to a man who couldn't even look his children in the face when they called me the best dad in the world.

A moral paradigm upon whom they could use as the template for their own future spouse. The world's greatest father, like it said on my coffee mug, the one who had all the answers and who lives a life as an example for others to follow. The church goer. The man who read all the books on religion and philosophy. The deep believer with an unwavering conviction which they admired dearly. In their eyes, that was me, that was I.

Not that most of that wasn't true. It was all me, once upon a time. Being a lifelong critical thinker, my idea of religion was that knowing God was the knowledge of God through study and more study. Books and more books. Read and re-read the how and why and the hidden secrets within the obtuse conversations of the great minds of the ages all wrapped around the wisdom of the saints and holy scriptures. Read and re-read, a nightly event that went on for many years. Over and over.

Not to memorize lines that I could barf up at a moment's notice like a parroting televangelist but to study and understand every single thought that was ever thought and that somehow, would reveal God. In my logical way of looking at theology, studying about God would bring you closer to God.

Prayer was little more than an afterthought.

What was the basic foundation of belief if not finding proof of a higher power through another person's experiences? To me, studying about Eucharistic miracles was equivalent to believing them possible and therefore believing them to be real. If a spiritual event occurred to a historical saint, then it was worthy of belief. I was safe in this understanding because I had read enough correlated material to cross reference and cross examine any doubt. I was ready; my spiritual bank was overflowing with knowledge and therefore confidence.

Then God abandoned me. And all the words on the well-worn paper blew away like dandelion seed. Within weeks of the marriage breakup my spiritual bank was totally bankrupt. Usually most people find chaos the push they need to turn *towards* God, even if it is nothing more than the desperate act of a desperate skeptic. Even the skeptic looks up to heaven when there's nowhere else to look. My eyes went straight ahead. The books went under the bed. To be brought to my knees to ask God to fix what he himself had broken was unthinkable. God was a hypocrite. My God, it seemed, had all the rash qualities of the gods of Olympus. Pettiness, capriciousness, selfishness, vengefulness. Hollow statues. Empty words.

So why should I climb Mount Carmel to beg for something that I was told in an old book that He would freely give me? Knock and the door will be opened, ask and you will receive, beg and you will be disappointed. I always felt I did enough asking, enough opening of doors for ten lifetimes and now I was expected to throw myself at His mercy? Petty and cruel was my God, like Zeus, mocking my years of devotion to His writings and all the holy writers.

Gone was my celestial Holy Family, now replaced by something of my own design. A complex series of deceits and fabrications woven around a carnal need and the want of companionship. None of it resembled the ideal flawless triangle of the Holy Family but an unholy triangle of a man and his wife and another man.

This arrangement would continue for many, many years. We would meet as often as we could. Dinner or just a drink. A stroll, shopping, all the things normal couples do, albeit in a much shortened version of normal. All the sex would come along as well, as would strong feelings of love and genuine happiness when we were together. We enjoyed each other's company extremely and I missed the days when I didn't see her.

But divorce on her part was out of the question. She was also a Catholic, a church goer and fairly devout even in her sin, but that wasn't the reason. Family issues, money and an extremely dangerous and unpredictable husband prevented her from making the move. Any normal third person would run, not walk from such a tenuous situation but I didn't care. My desires were my focus.

Making excuses and creating reasons for doing what I did became much easier as time went on. A skilled liar can fool just about anyone. A liar like me schooled by the Devil can learn to fool himself very quickly. I did *his* work so well that I was completely convinced of a lack of consequences for my actions on earth, or anywhere else.

But there were periods when the forces of heaven exerted it's presence upon my soul. During these times of flowing grace, I could end the adulterous relationship and focus on my sin. Things became purer during those bouts of clarity. I would sit in my church attentively, with every reading, every sermon seemingly directed right at me as though God purposely arranged the Lectionary just to convict me with his word. And the word had its effect as I would run to confession in tears and become prayerful and deep in my connection with the Lord. It was real, not a grand gesture on my part to placate God with false contrition, but real sincere repentance. Not seeing her or talking to her made it simpler. A growing coldness between us helped to close the distance between myself and the Lord. Sitting with my thoughts in meditation really brought my situation into perspective. To be this broken, lost and cut off from Gods love and grace felt unbearable during these periods. How could I have allowed this to happen?

Yet when I was at the core of my marriage meltdown, I experienced similar periodic re-connections with God. How could I save my marriage? The idea that my marriage was repairable felt like something God would adjoin with, so I plunged into a calculated series of heavenly appeals. My mother's little blue Pieta prayer book came out of the drawer and I would recite the mystical prayers the appropriate amount of times required in order to invoke the magic .

Entreaties to Mary became many and heartfelt. She would protect my family. She was herself a mother after all, the Mother of all Mothers. She would save my marriage.

Hours would be spent in silence in empty churches where I would experience the most amazing feelings of peace. But answers to my marriage dilemma still escaped me. My all-out prayer assault on the pearly gates was not yielding the results I had hoped. My wife wanted something different, opposite from my idea of what God wanted. It didn't feel possible that God would allow this breakup to happen.

Then one afternoon, that all changed and I got an answer. A direct, unmistakable answer from God Himself.

✳

I always liked empty churches even after the breakup. They felt less judgmental and more approachable. I didn't like thinking about my affair when I went to meditate on my sin. It was inevitable. Even in the sacred and solemn confines of the great basilica, the agent of discourse could cast his influence. Drifting in an out of prayer, contemplation and sleepiness was the norm. Thoughts would float through my mind, of God, of my sins, of her soft nakedness, of my wanton desire, of contrition and guilt, all swirling about me like a swarm of confused bees. The head of Beelzebul.

III

GOD SPEAKS

When human beings find themselves in a moment of great crisis numerous outcomes can occur. Awareness, enlightenment, understanding, resignation, disbelief, denial, breakdown, madness, self-destruction and anything in-between. I experienced a little bit of it all and at one point much of it simultaneously. When my wife left, my world dissolved. Searching for answers became the mission. There had to be a reason for what happened, somewhere on a wrinkled, coffee stained page, an explanation was written out as to why God allowed this tragic circumstance to tear apart one of his sacred families. I searched and searched but not one author could reasonably convince me that the unfairness of life was really the fault of Adam and that I was nothing more than a casualty of original sin.

In the midst of this crusade for ultimate knowledge I would occasionally become deflated and turn my sorrow over to Mary. She became my retreat when knowledge became worthless. Shamefully, that was a resource that never stuck with me over the passing years. But during those early bouts with abject helplessness, my total capitulation to Gods primacy was real as was the love I felt for our Holy Mother. She saved me more than once with her mother's love.

I would visit a local basilica dedicated to her mother, St. Ann and spend many hours sitting in the empty expanse praying or meditating, my thoughts occasionally just drifting about, even dozing off at times. Sporadically, odd things would occur. Odd only in the sense of how they would occur at a particular time of need. I would wander into the very large empty church and sit about in random seats only to find a pamphlet or booklet dealing with divorce or loss; or go to light a candle and realize I had no money only to find the right amount of change sitting on top of the money box.

Small incidents of this sort happened more often than one would expect, unless you believed in something other than coincidence. But even the compiling of these numerous oddities didn't prepare me for a seismic heavenly intervention. A major league fast ball right at my head.

When a person tells you a story, it's nothing more than a good story no matter how fantastic it may sound. Big or small, if they are outside the normal scope of life then they are worth a telling. But until a particular event actually happens to you, there is always that personal disconnection.

One person can believe they saw a ghost, or another a flying saucer, all wonderful tales but until you actually see the little green men with your own eyes, it's only just a pleasing tale passed along by another.

Many a prophet heard the voice of God. The Bible is full of their accounts, and is stated as fact. Moses spoke to God as we all know, face to face. But does God always speak in a physical voice for the human ear to hear? We also know he can speak in the clap of thunder or a rush of the wind. He also reveals his intentions to the mind's eye as he did with Moses.

In truth I never understood any of that. God's voice, a rush of wind? Did he sound loud and brash or was his voice low pitched and soft? To me this all sounded ridiculous, as did the idea of people claiming to have a revelation of the mind.

For the most part any story is just another anecdote, a tale . . . until it happens to you and probably leaves more questions than answers.

And the tale always begins with a beginning something like this.

What follows is a true story, not just based on a true story. One breezy summer afternoon, on a day like any other day, I found myself at the basilica wandering about as I had done countless times before.

First I visited the large votive candle room in the lower level of the building to light a few colored candles. A beautiful room partitioned off from a chapel area, enclosed by glass windows and containing an effigy of Saint Ann. The glow of the many candles and the deep silence make it an ideal place to pray and reflect. Even the heavy smell of evaporating wax surrounded you with tranquility.

But this sunny day brought me back up to the main church level. A high arching ceiling and soaring marble columns give the room a vast coolness. The niche to the right side of the alter holding the life sized icon of Saint Ann and a young Mary glowed under the sunlight streaming in through an amber stained glass window. A life sized crucifix with corpus appeared to float under the large marble and plaster altar canopy. The inviting emptiness of the space created serenity and retrospect.

I always found the basilica an oasis for my mind. My thoughts of hopelessness would get lost inside the enormous structure and float up to the great ceiling. It was one of the few places where I was able to let go all of the anger and fear building inside me from my current separation and pending divorce. This day was like any other day. Just another quite, summer day, me sitting alone in a random pew, my eyes closed and my mind foggy and unfocused, with nothing but a slide show of non-descript thoughts rolling through my brain.

Just an hour before this I had spent time on the phone discussing the merits of my persistence in attempting to make the marriage work. I was convinced God wanted me to stay strong, stay the course, ride it out and be there for my family when it all got sorted. My wife would see the light. All of the pain, anger and frustration I was feeling was a cross I needed to carry but in the end it would be all worth it. God expected me to stay in line and to hold the family together. Wait her out and stay the course. God wanted us together. I was convinced of this plan and therefore I easily convinced the person on the other end of the phone of my plan of action. I was determined to weather this bad patch and wait for the better days to come.

So arriving at the basilica that day was really for a spiritual tune-up, an adjustment of the soul. There was no agenda of begging or pleading and assaulting heaven for intervention in my problem. I knew what I had to do, stay the course. It was just peace and calm that I needed that day. Sitting and drifting. Thinking about music or what I would have for dinner that night, thinking about nothing and letting the emptiness take me away from my strife.

My eyes stayed shut. Thoughts came and went, my mind relaxed almost to the point of dozing off. It was very quiet even outside the church. In the distance I could hear a car turning over its motor and I knew it was the 1969 Camaro Z28 that was down the hill that I would pass now and then. The rumble was unmistakable and I could picture the car, Daytona yellow with black stripes, the image of it jumping into my wandering mind. What a car.

Suddenly, shockingly, forcibly, in the midst of my Camaro dream, three words were struck into my brain cells. It was not a thought. It was not a memory. It was not an idea. It was not a mental recitation. It was not a voice. It was not a sound. It was not under my control but from beyond me. Yet three words, clear, strong, unmistakable and forceful, jarringly embedded themselves into my mind as if someone ran wires into my brain and forced the recognizable syllables in against my will. Just three simple words.

"LET HER GO."

It was like a bolt of lightning energizing the grey matter in my skull. Zap. Kablam. The words just implanting themselves causing me to straighten up in the pew with a start. What in the heck was that, I thought, what just happened? Nothing in the church was out of place. No one was around. All was silence but my body was electric and all nervousness. I looked around panic stricken. Something just happened outside my realm of control. I could not stop it even if I knew it was about to happen.

I was like a puppet. Did I just receive some sort of a message? Where did it come from and why? I felt small and vulnerable, totally vulnerable. I kept looking all around, completely spooked.

Up and out of the church I went, down the limestone stairs and dashed off to my car. The gas pedal went down and I blew out of the basilica parking lot like a carnival clown shot from a cannon. My mind was racing. Let her go, let her go, let her go. What, how, why? What the? What could this mean?

This 'message', if that's what it was, was completely in contrast to my attitude, to my plan. It was NOT what I would be thinking or asking God to confirm. In truth, it was the total opposite, a 180 degree shift from my focus. It was *not* the answer I'd been praying for all those long months. Being a dedicated husband and father meant putting up with all the pain and misery in order to save the marriage, not to give it up. But these words were crystal clear and unmistakable. Let her go.

While driving, I suddenly became aware of what it meant. Not only where the words clear but so was the meaning behind them, which in itself was a very strange thing. Should I be scared, angry, confused . . . or should I be resolute? My future would lead in another course.

By the time I reached my house, a weird calm came over me. It had all become clear. There was no confusion about what I should do going forward as far as my wife was concerned. It was so bizarre but there it was. My direction changed, just like that. I can't explain it and I can't deny it.

Following this event I was determined to let her go, whatever that meant, however it had to be done, whatever the cost. It meant giving up the dream of having my family back, all of us living under one roof. It meant a fractured life, kids coming and going with two homes and getting on different school buses and all the other crap that comes with that sort of a situation. And yet I was OK with it. Not totally, not without remorse and guilt that I would let my children down.

I still felt all those feelings and anger of course. But it also felt that a direction was chosen and a path shown. Why this particular path I did not understand and maybe, I never would. My hope, however, was that God would eventually reveal to me the reason for this direction. Was there to be something else for me, another goal or circumstance more suiting.

This event launched me into a period of immense grace and new worlds seem to open up before me. My connection with the Lord was never stronger even in the middle of a family dissolution. My prayer life was stronger, my devotional life was stronger, my relationship with my Catholic faith exploded, I went to more masses, said more novenas, read more books on the Devil, Heaven, Hell, mysticism, the saints, the popes, apologetics, religious history, got involved in Catholic blogs and chat rooms, volunteered more, proselytize more and on it went. It was a divine explosion.

Then one day I discovered something interesting in regards to spiritual warfare. A bit of odd information. First I read about it, and then later I would experience it firsthand.

There was this great battle raging above the earth and on the earth and below the earth, the great conflict for our souls, being waged in a decidedly underhanded way by the Prince of Lies. And one of the reoccurring themes within this battle was this; the closer one gets to the truth, the harder the enemy tries to confuse you and win back your soul.

Obviously the enemy has no need to bother waging war on those who live their lives blind and in the dark, but the people who are aware can see the truth, the truth of God's grace. But seeing the truth is also the trigger.

Then, the problem becomes discernment. For some of what we see isn't always what we believe it to be. At times, it can be the opposite. The physical world is easily manipulated. At these times, the Blind Guide is at work, taking us by the hand and leading us from the light into the shadow.

This explained a lot. For it appeared I was possibly under assault. At first I didn't put all the clues together but soon it became apparent. The Devil did not take kindly to my digging and probing for the truth. The truth of the Church and all it was and all it stood against was an affront to Hell and Hell decided to fight back. The truth of the risen Christ was an abomination to Hell and Hell decided to fight back. Push me back into the darkness.

So the battle commenced and I found myself ill equipped to fight this type of dark guerilla warfare.

*

Sex is a powerful drug. Chemistry mixed with personality. Who was I to fight it? Even the voice of the Almighty wasn't strong enough to diffuse the bomb inside me. Pushing through His wall of grace became the new obstacle to clear. Getting laid was the end game and admitting that it was, was the beginning of the end. No one should underestimate the power of our reproductive cravings. The Saints didn't deny it. They beat themselves raw trying to conquer it. God created this drive in mankind for its temporal survival and it thrives in all of us. Something as basic as human hormonal compulsions is easily manipulated by the Great Manipulator. It almost seems unfair that the odds are mechanically, chemically stacked against us by our own Creator. Why would I expect a hallowed mind explosion from the Holy Spirit to change anything? Pigs wallow in the mud because they like it. It's part of their nature. I was wallowing in sin; it was part of my nature. God so willed it.

IV

SATAN SPEAKS

THE MORNING STAR, THE Bringer of the Light, The Shining One, First Prime of the Most High, Greatest of the Fallen Angels, Father of Lies, The Evil One, King of Hell, Master Deceiver, Old Nick, Old Scratch, the no good bastard. Whatever you call him, he's factual. As in real, exists, tangible, true, and any other synonym you can come up with. There is a Devil, whatever that is; a cast out angel, a basic raw spiritual evil or an ugly creature with horns and a forked tail. This thing and its minions are omnipresent. They are around every corner ready to use every form of communication to confound and confuse. They are a general part of everyday life on this plane of existence. Why God allows them to wage war for our souls has never been properly explained, at least to me anyway. But make no mistake. The Dark Master is watching and waiting, waiting for the opportunity to whisper his lies into our mind. Twist a situation. Poke a problem. Throw someone off course. Torment the unstable. Torture the insane. Lure us with false promises that have too many strings attached. The gullible and the smart all fall sooner or later. It's just a matter of how far you fall.

And I would fall all the way to the bottom of the smoldering pit.

The pit is deep and the road to the pit is paved with deceptions of fool's gold. There is nothing true or enduring along this road. Nothing. And again, one more time, nothing. For quite a few years, just prior to and after my divorce I arrogantly assumed myself to be ascended to a higher level of spirituality. I wore a dazzling suit of armor, the breast plate of the Lord. My religious conviction had become so strong after my encounter with the mystical voice of God that the idea of anything piercing that armor was unthinkable.

At the time it was reasonable to believe that I was out of the woods, that the anger towards God that I had first felt when my family split up was now totally healed. And moving forward had become effortless. This time, I was safely tucked into Gods hands and this time he wouldn't let me go.

The problem is that arrogance will cause you to lose your sight. And a blind man will hold out this hand to be led about. Loneliness can become a powerful ally of the Evil One and he will use it to lead you onto that road to the pit. In my case it was almost too easy. Sooner or later I would jump onto his road and run along towards my ruin. The suit of armor would fall away as easily as a snake losing its skin. Shred with ease.

But at the height of my zeal I was resistant to his advances. My resistance was met with continuous attacks. The Devil and his cadre didn't hesitate to show their intentions and it was an all-out combat for my soul. Evil didn't care to hide itself in subtle nuisances and whispers but came at me full on. The more I prayed the more obvious the attacks. I started having horrible dreams. Dreams of demons, of weird sexual situations, of being held down by something and unable to move while being assaulted. Occasionally I would have dreams of relatives that had passed on appearing to be warning me of something unsure. Bizarre dreams, of falling, of being chased. It wasn't a nightly event, but certainly a few times a week. This was something I had never encountered. It scared me.

But dreams weren't the only odd bit of circumstances. Once, near the outside door of the basilica I was met by an older woman, who looked sadly at me and just casually said, "whatever you think is in there, it's all a lie," and then walked off. This really disturbed me.

Books would go missing, religious medals would be misplaced.

I even had an incredibly frightening problem with my computer, also another strange and real event.

One night, while searching for travel information for a planned trip to Ireland, the first set of search results came back as 'sex with demons'. I was startled. How looking for travel information to Ireland could become 'sex with demons' was astonishing. Deleting the search bar and re-typing my travel query, the result came back this time as 'demon sex'. Not quite the same wording but obviously in the same search group. This really shook me. What the heck was this all about?

Going into the browser I erased all the cookies and search inquires, even to the point of looking into the Windows system files. Pornography, truthfully, was not something I ever looked at and there would be no possible reason for this to come up. After erasing all the prior search information I once again typed in travel to Ireland and once again the results came back as 'demonic sex acts'.

This time I was out right scared, creeped out to the point of looking warily around the room and talking to myself. I got up and waked into the kitchen, but feeling like I wasn't alone in the house. The television went on to ESPN for about an hour and a few causal phone calls were made to family members before returning to the bedroom.

Was I being dared to click on that link, to see what 'sex with demons' could possibly be? Instead, I said the Saint Michaels prayer fervently out of fear. Not once but twice. Out of fear. Then when I typed in my travel search inquiry again, all the normal travel information came up about Galway and Limerick but nothing sinister.

Now I was really spooked and I mean spooked. There it was in plain sight. No curtain to hide behind, no mask. The demons didn't care that I knew they existed, they only wanted to intrigue me just enough to not care about the consequences of clicking that link. Over and over they tried to entice me but I resisted. This event was so unnerving that the possibility of me being fooled into being a sinner was unimaginable. I was strong. I passed the test.

As fantastic as this all appears, it was factual. I was not emotionally compromised, nor hallucinating, nor was I a believer in the occult or magic or even demons for that matter, not in the everyday sort of way. And I never felt myself particularly enamored with spiritual magic or tales of miracles. These types of odd metaphysical events were not something I was particularly aware of. Then they just happened and eventually I began to realize they were all connected.

Satan wanted to rattle me. The deeper I pushed into the truth, the more he reared his ugly head. And I was rattled, to the marrow. What an eerily unnatural and unexplainable thing to happen. But regardless of how severe or outrageous the attack was I would not break rank from his full frontal assault. The Devil had to out flank me, come at me from another side or from the rear with a less obvious plan. We all know he is the master exploiter. And in the end I would be exploited, freely and willingly. He didn't need to scare me, just offer me something nice and juicy, like bait for the fish.

A few months after the computer event I experienced a setback in my relationship with my now at this time, ex-wife. Feelings of anger, frustration and loneliness pushed me into an emotionally depressed state. And it wasn't long before the whispering voice started making suggestions in my ear. Usually during my lunch hour I would take a walk at a local park. So did the company secretary. Soon we would go together.

It wasn't hard to become attached to her. She was a special person, the type of person everyone loved. Kind, sweet, generous, even tempered, gracious, a giver. She was also petite and attractive. Married to ogre of a husband, she suffered through years of neglect, drinking, viciousness and abuse. And this made her obtainable.

It also wasn't hard for her to become attached to me. I can be a gentleman, especially when compared to her husband and also a kind and giving person. She saw in me a good father, a smart, attentive friend; someone who was easy to be around and generally an all-around really nice guy.

Completely true. And we enjoyed each other's company. It was easy to have a heartfelt conversation between us. Over a short period of time, sharing our troubles and woes allowed us to become emotionally connected. Soon this would lead to holding hands on our walks, then a kiss, then many kisses and then eventually sex. And more sex. A very happy progression and very satisfying.

These encounters were actually wonderful and I looked forward to our time together. There is no point in not admitting this truth. Regret doesn't change the past or the facts. It was good, really good. And as time moved along, my faith slipped farther and farther into the background. Sin covered everything around me. Losing any feelings of a pious guilt allowed the moral part of me to wither away. This transition happened rather quickly, the armor falling away like dander.

It's amazing how fast years and years of devotion can disappear under the pressure of desire. I thought I was invincible but I was exposed as a fraud. I knew all the prayers, all the words but never understood the heart of the word.

When my move to a life of sin was totally and freely undertaken and I had done so of my own accord, ALL of the peculiar or supernatural events stopped. No more dreams of demons, no more being chased or held down, no more waking in a cold panic, no more weird voices, no more strange encounters with random people, no more disappearing bibles, no more demonic computer searches.

And no Godly encounters either. Nothing. In fact, my life became so worldly and normal that I almost forgot any of those things ever happened. The voice of God I heard in the basilica that wonderful summer day now faded away to the point of me questioning if I imagined the whole event. Satan had succeeded in filling my mind with doubt and apathy. The noise of everyday life, of television and sports and working and cars and money and cutting the grass was all that there was. I was moving through time, doing what we all do. Get up, go to work, eat, sleep, get up and do it all over again with an occasional adulterous interlude thrown in for good measure.

I was distracted by my stuff. And that was exactly how Satan wanted me; too busy to think, to question, to pause, to look behind the curtain. It was like being a character in a book but not being aware of it and thinking that everything around you is all that there was to life.

The book I was now a living part of was written by the Father of Lies. Nothing was true and it all led to nothingness.

✳

Every action begets an opposite reaction. She told me that she was going on vacation with her husband, their annual trip to his brother's house down south. This was not new. They'd taken this trip every year for as long as I'd known her, many years longer than our entanglement. Mostly he'd just sit around, drink and ignore her. But I realized of course that he'd press her for a bit of sexual doings; it was his vacation after all. Every year he'd drag her on this trip and every year I would get jealous and angry over it. Every year she'd tell me she was going and every year I would imagine the big soft bed at the vacation home. This is the essence of adultery in its matured form. Once the excitement of the naughtiness is over, once the exhilaration of the crime is past, then you've lasted long enough to actually start caring about one another. Soon the reality of the situation starts to sink in. The truth of what's actually going on; the fact that you're sharing another person emotionally and physically with someone else. But what did it matter. In the end he got what he wanted, when it wanted it. He was the husband and I was the interloper looking for whatever scraps remained unclaimed. Second fiddle in the sexual orchestra. What a rotten place to be and yet, there I was. He got what he wanted and I got whatever was left over but that was good enough for me.

V

TWO SIDES

Today it is common to view our modern existence as one big 'gray area' and not in terms of black and white. Today there are no absolutes. There is no wrong or right, specifically. There is no good or evil, actually. There is only relativism. And this would be a lie.

Human conflicts can have many fronts, many sides, but the perpetual spiritual war that rages on all around us only has two sides. God's side and those who are not on Gods side. God and his heavenly hosts opposing the armies of Hell. Now one would assume this war to be completely lopsided. On one hand you have the almighty Creator, the one who brought his own enemies into their very existence and who presumably could un-create them with a mere word. And yet, he doesn't speak that word but allows the war to continue. A war not for land or power or money but for souls.

Why would he allow such a battle to press on and on as countless millions are swept up onto the conveyer belt towards hell, all through the guile and deception of a dark army?

Unfortunately that is something I could never grasp. The shear illogic of it is proof positive to the non-believer that God could not exist and that the ancient ideas of good versus evil are nothing more than archaic superstition. Bronze Age silliness, regurgitated Gnostic nonsense. This would make sense to anyone living a life with their head buried in the modern world. All of the white noise creates an illusion of the preeminence of man and scientific reason. But all that really is, is the diversion. A diversion to keep us from seeing the impending attack until it is too late.

Oddly many of these same people who would blindly deny God would certainly believe in ghosts or goblins.

What they don't understand is that it's actually not that hard to see the physically manifested side of the true spiritual realm, if you take the time to look. It's all around us and in many ways quite obvious. The more open you are to the truth the more the blinders fall from your eyes.

And the veil was pulled away from my face, I saw the ugly side. Yet I chose to put a veil back over my face and to see things slightly blurred.

Clearly another miscalculation. In the spiritual war, there are only two sides. You're on one side or the other, there is no middle ground. You're either with God or you are against God. Modern religion would like you to believe that this 'gray area' also exists somewhere between God and his enemies, a sort of spiritual neutral zone where we can step back and forth from one side to the other. Where we can be ignorant of whatever actions are truly sinful and therefore not really be responsible for those sins. Gray sins.

In the Gospel passages there is not much of a 'gray area', in fact it is just the opposite. When Jesus speaks about sin he speaks in absolutes. And the consequences are also as absolute. So why would God allow us to be lured and shuttled off into a life of sin and damnation without pushing back, without trying to take back what was His from the foundation?

The answer is He wouldn't. For every lie that is spun by the enemy, God abandoning us is the grandfather of all lies. God is the truth tenfold. For every evil whisper in your ear, there is a blaring of celestial trumpets. I heard them, many times, during my sojourn on the dark side of the war, calling me back over the line to the light. I ignored them.

I can recall vividly all of those moments sitting in Sunday mass when the Gospel reading appears to have been picked out especially for me; or seeing a television show that just happened to parallel my adulterous situation. I've even had random people bring up conversations about cheaters and cheating. This was totally indiscriminate as my affair was not known to anyone, not even our closest friends.

To count how many times these sort of occurrences transpired is impossible. More than once I was convicted by a strange circumstance immediately after one of our sexual rendezvous. There wasn't a week that went by that some article or story or email or movie or booklet would convict me. People could attribute this to the 'now that I have it' syndrome. Drive a certain type of car and suddenly they seem to be everywhere, when in reality, you just never noticed them. But this was not the case. These messages were deliberate and numerous, far more than me just never noticing all of the social material on extra-marital relationships.

It was personal. It was private. It was everywhere. It was God fighting back, blowing His trumpet in my face. I even had dreams about my affair and never the good ones. They always had a bad ending. Guilt could certainly cause a dream like that. But all those circumstances were consistent messages put into either a physical or supernatural action.

It would be a good wager to assume that many-many people in comparable situations to me have had similar odd experiences. As a matter of fact, you could count on it.

Attack and counter-attack was the name of the game. The most remarkable part was that neither side ever gave up on me. Never was there a point where it appeared God had enough of my nonsense and was throwing in the towel and letting the other side just stroll away with me arm in arm. He never gave up on me.

Conversely neither did God's adversary. And to be fair, Gods task was much harder than the Devils. God had to rely on appealing to guilt and good judgement and a sense of righteousness. The Devil relied on bared female breasts.

The Devil relied on the need for sexual intimacy and on others things such as loneliness and low self-esteem. All tangible and immediate human needs not easily slaked off by prayer and meditation. It's really not a fair fight. And since I was already living in the 'gray area' it made for no fight at all.

I strutted along the imaginary border between good and evil like a matador tempting a raging bull. In reality I wasn't on any border but squarely on the Devils side parading around like a fool. There is no 'going deeper' into sin. You cross the line and you're in. You can wander farther and farther from the border but the landscape is unchanged. One toe in is the same as a thousand miles down the road in perdition. It's all in or nothing in.

Still God fought the good fight. Constant road signs and loving nudges rolled along. Sermon after sermon about adultery or infidelity, about being a good husband or wife, about effects of sin on one's soul, about the dire consequences and blah-blah, did little to change me. Homilies, booklets, shows, conversations about having affairs or past affairs, it was endless. Yet nothing was going to stop me from having my lust satisfied and my emotional void filled. Nothing, nothing at all.

※

I tell her a joke and she laughs uncontrollably almost spilling her coffee. We've spent many hours like this in casual conversation, just enjoying each other's company. We belong together, we really do. I know it, she knows it. There is no anger or angst between us. We genuinely like each other, a lot. I take a sip of my coffee and tell her another stupid joke and she laughs again. Once the coffee is gone she has to leave. Forty five lousy minutes out of a life time. I get angry as she leaves the coffee shop. Why do I put up with this crap? She goes home to her husband and I go home to an empty house. I know what goes on at her house. Arguments, drunken ramblings and probably sex. He gets what he wants from her and I have to live with that reality. She won't spell it out, she hates him but she fears him. And somehow, I'm supposed to be OK with that.

She's getting 'laid' by another man, who just happens to be married to her. For a moment I forget, I'm the other man. The situation is so confused in my mind at times that the anger builds. I feel empty and lost. Why do I continue?

As I go to my car I notice a napkin under my windshield wiper with a heart drawn on it and suddenly the anger goes away. There are always two sides.

VI

LOVE

I LOVE YOU. THE great lie that washes a cheaters sins clean, like a great sparkling bapstism. Love can also be a problem, especially for someone who is having an affair. The last thing an adulterer needs is a strong emotional connection to their partner in crime. Sexual appetites are hard enough to control but adding in an emotional component totally changes the game. Where once boredom would compel you to end the relationship, love makes the relationship seem legitimate. It's the absolute worst thing that can happen to a cheater because now, you're justified. In time, you can almost convince yourself that you're doing the right thing and it's even something that God *wants* you to do. God wants you to be together, its fate and you are soul mates joined in the cosmic heavens only to be kept apart by an illegitimate marriage.

While the emotion may be real, the rest is not. It's total rubbish. It's the push by the king Pusher, using that emotion and then twisting it into a false truth, creating the lie and the fairy tale to lock down the contract. Any doubt you may have had on the reality of your treachery is now compromised. It could be very easy to convince yourself that God *wants* this affair and not only wants it, but blesses it. Yes, he blesses it and is in full agreement with the

Devil on this one. You both should be together, not apart. God wills it. The Devil wills it. I will it. We all agree.

But that's not all there is. There is more, much more. Love takes you deeper into the rabbit hole. The tales and lies created became epic Greek tragedies of lost love. I wanted it so, I willed it so.

I loved her; I believed that. That was not a hard thing to do as she was an amazing person. Saying that is not something I used simply to justify my actions but the real honest truth as I knew it. Anyone, everyone that knew her would not find that hard to believe.

She was great and good and special. She was a rare being, a kind, sincere, gentle, and overly giving woman and every other good thing you can imagine. And she was also an adulterer.

There would be some members in her family that would be ecstatic for her if they knew that fact; that she had found someone she cared about and found love and was happy. They wouldn't care that she had a husband since they all hated him and hated how he treated her. But none of them knew about us. One family member suspected we had a special connection but they didn't know how strong and how deep that connection really was.

Seeing her every day, having conversations about family issues, going over the news events, small talk, doing crossword puzzles at break time and all other manner of normal interaction built a friendship that only helped to strengthen our romantic bond. Our personal time together was even more intense. The sex was amazing and she had created enough chores, excuses and explanations to allow for her clandestine movements

We would meet in all manner of locations. It was all a wonderful game. Now, I stopped wondering what would happen if her husband found out about us or what my own children would think about their father, the saint, the church goer, the guy who has piles of religious books stacked all over his bedroom, the person who hangs pictures of Mary and various saints all over the refrigerator.

I knew I was a fake, a fraud, a phony. Yet, in my contaminated mind and wretched soul I was a still very devout man. Attending prayer vigils, rosary recitations, Monday evening masses would somehow overshadow this one glaring fact. That I was a cheater, a commandment breaker.

Love was the great binder; it brought it all together, the good and bad. So being in love meant Christmas gifts, birthday gifts, setting up dinner dates, hiking, shopping and all the many assorted things that 'couples' do. Except we weren't a couple, not really.

A true couple lives through the bad times as well as the good, which means fighting, family problems, money issues and dealing with everyday life on a regular basis. We shared none of those experiences. What we shared was a shallow, thinned version of real life. What this assumption of being 'in love' accomplished was to push the guilt sideways. People in the midst of an illicit relationship often adopt this common justification and in many cases it works in convincing the perpetrators that their liaison is acceptable on a very deep emotional level. We bought into this scam with reckless abandon.

Within every game there are kernels of truth of course, sometimes more than one. We did have those feelings for each other. She was badly treated in her marriage. If circumstances were altered, had she left her husband years prior or he died or moved to the Yukon in search of gold, then the outcome would have been different. The relationship would then have the chance to be proven solid in the way that all relationships are proven solid; by spending a lot of time together and finding out if you were actually in love and compatible. Or it would fall apart all on its own.

There was a good chance that we were highly compatible. But we'd never be able to put that to the test. She could never leave him and that left us with our only option. To sneak around and to lie; lie to ourselves and everyone we knew. Make up stories and excuses. Take risks. Tell more lies.

Sadly, proclaiming to each other that we were in love was our biggest lie to each other. Because the reality of it was that even if that was truthful on the surface, true love would have meant letting each other go. But lust and neediness meant more than truth. Immature feelings of love meant more than actually being in love and doing the right thing. God told me to let my wife go, but what about now?

They say God is love. So how could anything we were involved in have anything to do with love, it certainly had nothing to do with God. It also had nothing to do with being a Catholic. I knew enough of the Catechism to know just how far out of bounds this all was. I actually taught Catechism for ten years. I preached and pranced about the classroom acting the classic role model. Pointing and drawing diagrams on the blackboard to illustrate the fall from Eden to the 7 year olds. To the 10 year olds I explained how God made saints out of sinners using Saint Peter and Saint Paul as the grand examples. The denier and the oppressor.

Was the promise of a good roll in the sheets all that it took for me to make mistake after mistake? God wanted me to listen. He begged me to listen, sending ample messages via his messengers, one after the other and I turned them all away. Strolling out of Gods Garden was easy, especially when accepting a self-imposed lie such as being in love. The irony of love being used against God's love.

If anyone actually thought about what they were doing in committing adultery, it makes no sense, not really. Unfortunately, we are all creatures of this mortal world and therefore subject to its definitions of wants and needs.

Passions and wants and desires are real. They are part of our DNA, since the beginning, since that first fruit was plucked by our ancestors. Humankind was made to live, to want to live, to carry on and spread across the face of the world. It is a very difficult task to fight off desires and lust regardless of any religious parameters. Just because God or a Pope or a priest or a pastor or even your best friend can say 'no don't do that', the primordial chemicals swirling inside our brain can stimulate us into making decisions totally contrary to our personal beliefs or innate personality. You can find yourself doing things you never thought were possible.

The creatures of the spiritual realm are immune to such things as raging hormones. Our hope to attain that sense of total detachment from earthly devices is something we can only look to attain in heaven, where we will be free of all governing mortal passions. But not free of emotion. No, for God is love and love is the most powerful of all emotions. Some would like to say that anger is or hate, but both anger and hate are only branches of the much deeper emotions, usually fear or envy or self-loathing.

The higher creatures of the spiritual realm truly are immune to the confines of human emotions and sexually but the evil creatures are not and will always use those frailties against us.

And they did and what did I have as a result? I love you and you love me, so let's go find a place to have sex. Shallow and sad and nothing more than window dressing to allow my mind to not accept who I was and what I was doing. Nothing more than an aid in justifying walking away from God and walking into a dank smelly motel room near a strip mall.

It's hard to come to terms with the fact that we really know nothing. It's always a shock when we find out the truth.

We erroneously trust in our own intellect, in the myth that we have it all figured out and that all the theories and all the discussions taking place in all the university's around the world have worked out all of creation and every truth contained in it and outside it. And the things we don't currently know are nothing more than the things we haven't discovered yet.

And this trust in humankind's primacy rules all our understanding, until it doesn't. Until the day something truly unexplainable happens, something that doesn't fit into a man-made construct. Like having the same dream five nights in a row, or seeing the same unknown person standing in a crowd, looking at you, at various locations or finding the same book on adultery in a pew in three different churches.

Catholic history is replete with irrational pious events. Weeping statues, bleeding hosts, signs in heavens, signs in the clouds, dancing suns, Mary appearing hither and yon with portents of the future, miraculous miracles, unexplainable healings and a cast of Saints that have done everything from levitate to being in two places at the same time. Generally most of these spectacles got ignored by everyone outside of the truly faithful. But it is a massive body of evidence, a sphere of influences spanning over 2000 years. Even taking into account some misrepresentation of certain events and any normal ancient myth building, what remains is inexplicably incredible. To learn about all this phenomena should conjure wonder and awe and hopefully righteous fear into every believer since so much of it goes against reason and it's impossible to doubt that Gods hand is extended over time and space and everything and everyone. But you can doubt if you try hard enough. You can ignore 2000 years of mysterious happenings if you look the other way or don't read that story or just don't care.

You can have an affair if you allow the sensual world to obscure the truth. And unfortunately, love is the twist. Love can open a door or lock a door. I chose the latter. My misuse of love locked God out of my heart. Some people say that love can never be a bad thing, that love is always necessary and good. That we can never have enough love.

This is simply not correct. Saint Paul said that love does not seek its own interest. That is a complete and absolute certainty, correct in every way. That is the true heart of love. Obviously, I was not in agreement with Saint Paul. My true heart was to be found much lower on my anatomy.

Our love was a contrivance, even if real in some nature, yet still a contrivance. It allowed us to do the things we wanted, a sort of free pass to break the law, like a Bishop giving a dispensation to Irish Catholics to eat all the ham and cabbage they want if Saint Patrick's Day falls on a Friday during lent.

Our love was a dispensation to break the Law of Moses. And break it we did, with many heartfelt 'I love you' moments and long kisses.

God watched in digust I am sure, for He has seen this rerun B movie many times before; two of His creations, using the same old excuses and following the same old pathway to ruination, one that many have used and many still are. The wide and very crowded pathway into the abyss.

✳

"I love you," she whispers to me as we lay in bed, "more than you can imagine." I reply in kind. And I mean it, whole heartedly. I still get nervous whenever she comes to my house. I can visualize the hubby's car pulling into my driveway, guns a-blazing. Yet somehow I don't care. She is kind and gentle and I want to spend the rest of my days hearing her tell me that.

But we have to dress quickly. The clock is running. An hour here, two there, excuses that must fit into the timeline of where and when. I take her back to her car parked behind the restaurant, let her out and then drive away, always glancing in my rearview mirror to make sure I'm not being followed. Every time the experience is the same and yet I go back and do it all over again. It's a fool's move, done by a fool.

VII

SACRED LESSON

WHY IS IT THAT a human can ignore warnings signs when they don't contain the message they hope to see? To be consciously aware of an action is to be responsible for any reaction one might experience related to it. It really is that simple. Once you 'know', you're on the hook to make the right choice or else. Once the teacher explains it, you can't say you weren't told. You can try to say you forgot the lesson or you didn't understand it or you can pretend to ignore it. But you were told. And being told more than once is the added weight around any false pretenses.

There is no greater teacher than God. He is truth and knowledge and purity of being. So when he takes the time to give us a lesson, it is a lesson worth studying and learning. Not only sometimes, but always. He is also patient and will show us the same lesson over and over and over and over. Only the tragically mentally impaired or hopelessly unintelligent can be forgiven the lack of comprehension. The rest of us, cannot.

I am not that stupid. But I am self-deluded and can fool myself into thinking that I could not see the sign posts planted squarely in front of me. I am that arrogant and will pretend to have never gotten the message, to have never seen the lesson.

The television is on and I am scrolling through channels, bouncing from program to program which is the usual nightly routine. On one major network, the plot is about how a man in Chicago is tracking his wife's phone that he believes is having an extra-marital relationship. I casually scroll down the channel list until I see another program that gets me to stop at a movie that I'd never seen before. The scene is showing a man and woman having a clandestine rendezvous at a mountain cabin.

Again the causal scroll now stopping at EWTN, where there is a 15 year old program featuring Mother Angelica talking about infidelity of all sort in her usual candid and forthright manner, bouncing one hard blow after another off my hard head. Once more I flip, this time to a baseball game, thus successfully completing a zig-zag all along the channel guide, dodging every sign post with dexterity and skill. I am not that oblivious, I am just ignoring the lesson and the sign post. The teacher told me and now I have to make the choice. I was made aware and now I will choose.

I chose her. Many others will make similar choices. The wide path is crowded with the people who ignore the sacred lessons and make their own wrong choice. On the narrow path are the ones who admitted that the sacred lesson was God's voice crying, "My child, listen to Me, I am coming to you as something familiar from your world to help correct you on your journey. I am not coming to you in a clap of thunder or a blaze of lighting or a rush of wind, but in the voice of reason through an old television program or through a radio show. I'm coming to meet you on your own plane of attentiveness, through the media you so crave. I've come down meet you, to be found in the appropriate timing of some random movie dialogue or magazine article. Are you there?"

I do hear you and I do see you. And I gaze right through you Lord, as if I am looking through a window at some coveted object beyond the glass pane. This reveals the second great lie after adulterous love, which is adulterous ignorance. There is no ignorance in sin, not really. You sin because you know the difference and still choose to do it.

Now the radio is playing as I drive to work. A local talk show blathers on in the background as I sip my coffee and watch the trees go by. One of the talking heads blurts out a reference to some recording artist I've never heard of recently being caught in a love triangle. Four days later, I stand at the back of my local parish church listening to my priest comment on the different understandings of the Greek word 'porneia'.

More lessons from the teacher, constant and never ending. Reaching out on the most human of terms, not in a lofty unfathomably way. Not as a pillar of fire but in an off-hand comment or side remark. To think about what is actually happening should strike fear and awe in any reasonable person, especially a Catholic. Catholics, as do some other Christian denominations understand the power of the spiritual realms. Not spirituality, but the actual tangible spiritual world we can't always see. It is there and it is real and from time to time we are allowed to peak beneath the shroud that hides it, to witness it fully exposed. And it is full of the blazing power and the amazing glory of God, as well as the lurking corruption of his opposition. It's full of wonder and miracles and hope and subterfuge and conspiracy and desolation. Of signs and of sacred lessons. A true Catholic really has absolutely no excuse for ignoring any of this

This spiritual world, from a Catholic perspective, is much more than just the Evangelical notion for a singular relationship with the Lord, but a total cosmological connection with the Triune God through the whole of His creation, good and bad. To understand how it binds us all together, through his Angels and his Saints and even through the darker side of His creation. It's all there, with us every day. We are bound up with the light and the dark.

And to see Gods power exposed, in this expression of concern for my undeserved well-being, by Him constantly reaching out to me in a totally obvious, non-coincidental way should strike me with guilt and fear. These supernatural outreaches should shake me into conceding that God is real, that my actions are being noted and, since God is real, then there will be consequences to my actions. Therefore the only rational thing to do is the stop sinning, end the relationship and turn back to the Lord. Or face the music.

But a really deep sinner, a lustful earthbound pig who is ruled by mindless hormones and a petty willfulness can ignore all of hellfire if it means one more go-round of sweaty sex. All the sacred signs and sacred lessons are just particles of sand blowing about, here and there and everywhere.

So what is the truth? What is truth? "Quid est veritas?" Three of the most famous words in all of recorded human history. Jesus never answered Pilate the way he expected. Pilate was blind to the truth that was standing right in front of him, God's living grace, staring him right in the face. Pilate saw only a man and nothing more. Any answer that Jesus could have given would have fallen on a deaf ear. The teacher had already spoken his lesson, over and over. Now it was up to Pilate to make his choice. He chose.

What is truth? Truth is the opposite of a lie. A simple yet all-encompassing answer. Truth doesn't take sides, nor is it always holy. To live in a sin can also to be living in a truth. If you embrace your sin, not everything about it is a lie. I am a sinner. Truth. I will not change. Truth. I knowingly ignore God's entreats. Truth. I understand the consequences but chose to continue in sin. Truth. I am a worm and no man. Truth.

But what did Jesus mean by saying "I am the truth?" That statement is very different from what Pilate asked Him. God's truth embodies what it means to be part of salvation history. Jesus' bold statement of his own truth was much bigger than anything Pilate could ever imagine. Pilate said, "Ecce homo", "behold the man." What he didn't realize was that he was actually referring to himself, not Christ.

Pilate's idea of 'truth' was our truth, man's truth, a sinner's truth, my truth . . . earthbound, simplistic and based on human perspectives. So for mankind, sin can equal truth. In God, there is no sin. He is all love, filial love and the answer to every question, even Pilates.

Pilate handed him over. He had him scourged and crucified; just as I had done every time I cheated. I was the deceiver and the cheater, an adulterer lashing away with my actions at Christ's body chained at the pillar. Aware of this horrible prospect, I still pressed onward. Driven by my desire, I ignored the lessons being communicated to me almost daily. My will be done.

I want what I want. And I wanted her. Nothing short of her raging husband was going to stand in my way, certainly not the replaying ramblings of an old nun on some television program or a coincidental Sunday sermon. I wanted my sex. My steamy passionate sex. Call it what you will. Making love, getting it on, whatever, it was great. I thought about it. I dreamt about it. The devil never let it slip far from my mind's eye. I could smell it, taste it. The very meaning of being an animal on a planet teeming with animals. It was natural. Without it we would cease to exist. The drive was something built into us from scratch, poured into the gene pool by God Himself at the moment of divine creation, whether in Eden or at the dawn of our primordial ooze.

If anyone was to blame for my actions, it was the Creator who made me so flawed, so abjectly tied to this function. All the pious words and good intentions of countless saints could not just wash away our very nature. Saint Paul may have wished it to be so, but even he had to concede that not everyone could be like him and should give in to their human cravings. I was simply following that example.

Sort of. I was certainly following my human cravings, while ignoring all the structure that surrounded it. For as in all things human, a structure must be built up, lest our very nature destroys us. The seven deadly sins, the eight beatitudes, the twelve commandments. The Mosaic Law, the Golden Rule. All of these should come with a warning label. 'Practice these guidelines or perish by your own hand.' The Sacred Lessons. Not to be ignored, for if you do, proceed at your own peril.

※

A text message chimes on the phone, an emoji of a heart and a happy face. I smile. It makes me feel warm inside. I want to text her back but I dare not respond.

Even after many warnings about texting she still sends them now and then. I wish there were more, could be more. I do miss her. I do love her. I want to be with her. I do crave the sex but it's more, much more. We're like two of a kind. She's wonderful, probably the kindest and most giving woman I've ever known and I want to spend all my time telling her this, telling her how I admire how she cares about others. To make her happy would bring me endless happiness. We could talk, take walks, tell bad jokes and laugh at each other. Or just sit on beach and let the wind wrap us up, this along with many other hopes we've dreamt about over the years.

None of this will happen. There will be no sitting on a beach, no long romantic conversations about our future. There is no future. Only a transfixed moment, frozen by a bad marriage to a wild man. Only a sad situation glued together by sin and lust and nothing more. Aspirations and hopes are meaningless and have no merit. Nothing but wishful thinking between two lovers who have little else but the back seat of a car. It almost feel tragic, Shakespearian in a sense. And it is. On a human level it truly is. Two people who so much want to be happy and together.

But is truth based on happiness? Truth is the opposite of a lie, not the opposite of unhappiness. And the only way for me to live in the truth, is to be unhappy.

VIII

A POINT OF VIEW

To be a real cheater is to be in the game longer than a one night stand. To a real professional cheater a one night stand doesn't count for much. And be a real cheater is to have a certain point of view. Not all are the same perspective, but every cheater has one. I had one and she had one. Mine was that I deserved someone finally, who truly loved me; hers was that she deserved some genuine and well-earned personal happiness. We both 'deserved' what we got out of that relationship; it was owed to us because we were previously cheated by fate.

People can conjure up all sorts of reasons, points of view for what they do and why. If you play the game long enough, you need to. Rest assured, most reasoning's can't simply rely on the desire for sex. After enough time has passed between two people that simply won't do as a motive to be carrying on an affair. You need more of a justification for your actions than just wanting a good romp with someone else's husband or wife.

My justification was that I was loved, wholly and truly for the first time in my life and I deserved to be loved. My previous relationships turned out to be false and hurtful. She wasn't like that. She was kindness and caring. The only similarity between my past relationships and my affair was that both were entwined with lies.

Strange as that may appear, it's the common thread. The past was hard and sad and blown apart by lies and the affair was soft and loving and held together by lies.

The simple inevitability of living in the mortal world is this; once you choose to operate outside of God's Law, everything begins to fall apart. Stray off the narrow path just a little to the left or right and the claws of the devils many helpers are there to put you on the wider path before you realize it. Everything we do and say to justify sin is nothing but a fake construct built on lies in order to confuse the truth. But happily, this tangle of lies provides you with the reason, the point of view, the excuse you need to convince yourself that your sin is justified and not only justified but deserved, owed. You owe yourself that sin because somehow, God shortchanged you somehow, somewhere. It really is an impressive bit of deception, cunningly straightforward. Play up to a human ego and they will damn themselves almost every time. Convince someone that they got screwed or a raw deal and they will do just about any immorality with a clear conscious.

It's a weird thing, to be in love with another man's wife and not to feel guilt over him. Again from my point of view, he was a monster and didn't deserve any guilt. But there were struggles, when a moment of clarity shone the light of truth; this is what you are doing and it's wrong regardless of the reasoning. For me, it wasn't about guilt over what I was doing, especially to any one person including her husband. It was my own personal guilt, knowing, that God knew exactly what I was up to.

We both twisted in the wind when it came to justifications. She had hers, I had mine. They both worked as intended. We met up, we did what we did. We would leave feeling fine.

Only one other person knew about our relationship. A close friend of mine. He worked it all out years ago and there was no keeping the truth from him.

We were very careful about keeping things secret. Even after many years, no one knew about us. Hiding our activities became an art form. Disappearing for a few hours became easy. Tweaking schedules, hiding calls and texts and advanced planning all contributed to over a decade of amusing immorality.

We got good at finding our little corners of privacy. A bathroom stall at work, a cemetery parking lot, a blanket in the woods. No shame meant no boundaries.

Driven by lust, we rocked and rolled our way amongst any available time and space. What did it matter as long as we got what we wanted. And what we deserved.

Deserved. A rather broad and untenable point of view for a lowly human to have. God on the other hand has no point of view. He is view, all view. There is only sin or no sin. It is an unmovable truth rather than a point of view. Mankind takes that eternal truth and skews it into complicated definitions of what is and isn't sin. Mortal sin, venial sin, white lies, half-truths, aware or unaware, capable or not capable, eat this, don't drink that, hellhound or purgatory bound.

I'd like to believe that God allows us these machinations and applies his justice according to our own definitions. Of course this can't be correct. The Church can declare 'ex cathedra' and so I must accept it, in theory at least, rather than in real practice. In practice I accept none of it. I ignore it all. But ignoring these teachings is like ignoring a small mole that later turns into cancer that if untreated, will most likely kill you.

No criminal ever believes they will unquestionably be caught; otherwise they would not do the crime. If you knew positively, that your action will end badly, that beyond a shadow of a doubt it will fail, you wouldn't do it. At least, that would be the logical assumption. Rob a bank and go right into a jail cell. What would be the point, unless, you're doing it just for the fun of it.

This is where human fault, Adams sin, puts many on the road to ruin, which includes myself. We do things for no reason other than we just want to do it. Consequences can be obvious and dire, even inescapable and yet we do it anyway. Mix in a healthy amount of lust, longing and loneliness and it almost doesn't seem fair. Human weakness gives the devil way to much ammunition to use against us. To me, it always appeared God had the harder fight in the tug-of-war for our soul.

Was I worth His effort in that battle, even a most minuscule amount of time?

✳

From my point of view, not only did I feel that I was entitled to have this elicit relationship but neither did I really care what God thought about my actions. There were times of guilt but ultimately I spurned any idea of fault or guilt. Lust, longing, loneliness. All conspiring to cloud my judgment. The devil had little work to do, just give me the little push and send me on my way.

God did push back, now and then, just to remind me that he still cared, that he didn't give up. The odd coincidences. The near exposures. And as many others can surely attest, the weird dreams would also come along. Another point of view.

One very sultry summer night I had an odd dream that I was driving my car on a local street heading home. Off in the western sky the bright orange sun was setting, a scene I would observe many-many times along this route. But off to the left of the sun, was another sun or disc of some sort. This 'sun' was a negative image, all blacked out in the center with a bright corona around it. A dark mirror. It pulsed and throbbed, similar to what I believe had happened at Fatima. People stopped their cars to gaze at the beating disc. I could see fear and confusion on their faces. I also stopped to look, half way across a large bridge that spanned the Susquehanna River, where I could see a clear view of the event downstream. Suddenly black clouds surrounded the negative sun, but not the real sun. The real sun still gleamed like on any other late afternoon summer day. People began to run back to their cars in fear. Soon heavy pellets of rain began to fall from the black cloud, directly at the bridge. As they struck the ground, they exploded like fire crackers. Quickly I rolled up my window and began to speed off, the pellets exploding on the hood of my car. Even though I knew it was a dream, I was still aware that this was an apocalyptic moment.

I drove off the bridge like a wild man, just barely missing another car. Then suddenly I awoke with a jolt, startled and shaken.

It was so real, not like a dream but sharp, clear, in living color and totally perceptible. It was like being an actor in a movie. Hours would go by before I could shake off the feeling and the sensation caused me to have a bit of inward reflection but by that afternoon, all that sensation had passed. After all, it was just a weird dream.

Was it a memo? Was it a slap in the face? Or was it just some altered dreamscape and nothing more than a splash of color from some random neuron fed broth? 'More gravy than of grave' as Scrooge believed of his spirits. I've never come to a conclusion as to what it was all about. I'd like to say for certain that it was of supernatural origin. But who could ever be sure of such things.

All the bad dreams occurred in my saintly days. Dreams of being chased by demons. Dreams of floating up from my bed and then falling down a long tunnel towards darkness. Dreams of people whispering horrible things to me while being held down in bed unable to move. Dreams of trying to run while being held at the ankles by unseen devilish hands. The whole gamut. Obviously these dreams were not every night and were spread out over years and years, but horrible enough to be clearly remembered.

And I'm not lunatic or nervous crack pot or in any way detached from a normal state of mind. The truth is I'm quite average and unassuming in many ways, but not alone in these experiences. Reading, research and inquiring around with other fellow Catholics and Christians led me to discover that many could tell similar stories, some more terrifying than my own.

For most it was the closer to the truth they got, the harder the other side came after them. Years prior, when my faith was going in the right direction, the devil worked me over fairly hard. But I was aware of it. It became so obvious that I was able to fight back.

Now I was way off the path. The Devil needed little interaction to keep me in his grasp for now I even doubted if God was even involved in my life. I could very readily believe that the Evil One was taking an interest in my soul, but not God. My blindness towards the fact that God was reaching out to me should have been a sign that the Evil One was working overtime. But by then, it really didn't matter. The devils goal and my goal were one in the same.

Everything mankind sees and does is from a perspective, a point of view. Change your point of view, change your reality. One man's sin is another man's triumph. But that was not God's way. Adam changed it all around, he charted a new way. And now I was making my own perspective. I 'deserved' this relationship and damn me either way, I was going to have it. And not only deserve it but here are the reasons that I do and the point as to how I am justified. Anyone who dare disagree with me just didn't understand the world from my perspective. That's all there is to it. If they did, they would agree with my decision. I was justified in what I did, they just didn't know it.

In actuality, that reasoning would only take place in my mind, an argument within an argument. No one, outside of one other person knew about the affair. I didn't have to convince anyone what I was doing was right, except me. So deserving the affair and my justified perspective was only constructed to justify myself to myself. Justification meant no guilt.

If something happened to cause me to rethink my wicked ways, my point of view would shift again. Just like that. Easy. Always justified. Any shift towards the good was fleeting, crushed again by lust, yearning and loneliness. Snuffed out, trampled underfoot like so many good intentions. And I had a few here and there, we all do. Yet, good intentions are just that. Intentions. Things we intended to do but have not done. Instead, we do something else.

I wanted sex. I wanted attention. I wanted companionship, even part-time. I wanted someone to care about me. I wanted an intimate friendship. I wanted gifts. I wanted sex.

And I got all that and more. More attention, more friendship and more sex than I could handle.

Was this healthy for me? It was what I wanted after all. And if you asked me that question my answer would usually be yes. But any rational person would just say that I could have all the things I wanted from a relationship without being involved with a married woman. Find someone else. Cultivate all those desires within the boundaries of an acceptable relationship. Totally sensible.

But I wanted her. I wanted what I wanted. And I got what I wanted. What did it matter what God wanted. We snuck around like rats in a sewer. Slippery eels, having our own way, acting like any other couple in love, just doing what any other couple would be doing. Everything we did, every place we went, every decision we made was based on our point of view. She was committed her to alibi. I was less committed to mine but committed enough to commit adultery, every single chance I got.

❋

I wasn't always like this. I wasn't always like this. I wasn't always like this. So what happened? How did I get so screwed up? Having a bit of unearned intellectual arrogance didn't help me. I was never a great student because generally school bored me. But I was always very smart, clever, able to see through situations, read people, sense attitudes, feel emotions, reason out someone's meaning and generally read minds. My mind was always crisp and able to put things together rather quickly especially when it came to complex ideas or theories. For some reason I had the innate ability to unravel complicated or obtuse explanations for everything from science to theology to politics. I was clever and keen eyed. And it gave me a false sense of wisdom, something that the devil would wield against me. Overly confident individuals are easy prey for the peddlers of immorality, since confident people are always blindly sure of their choices and decisions. They are never wrong. Confident individuals are some of the foremost creators of their own perspective and this is one reason why they are so confident. Like me.

She wasn't like that. She was kind and simple. She didn't over analyze or over think anything. In an odd way, she was actually closer to God than I was. Her life of pain caused her to act. My arrogance caused me to take advantage of that pain. And I knew deep down inside, this whole affair was on my shoulders. I created it.

IX

THE FACE OF DARKNESS

I HAVE SEEN THE face of darkness and it was mine. Bitter and twisted and dark. All about me was darkness from without as well as within. The without, being wholly of my own creation was apparent. Eyes collapsed upon themselves, blood shot, encircled by swells of skin. A grimaced look and a wince, then a whimpering falter, staring and angry and puffed up on adrenaline like some midnight movie show extra.

But the within, was also mine but also of another. Genuine fear becomes front and center with the sudden awareness of your own vulnerability, the human condition of the flesh, of the mind that is as easily moved along as a dandelion seed on the wind.

And it came to me, this darkness, one bad and awful night, in the middle of a breakdown and struck such fear in me to the point that the writing of these very lines fills these fingers with despair. This is no idle exaggeration, no hyperbole. It is fact and reality and truth and exact in its detail. It is not hallucination or transference. It is sadness and grief and shame and abject dread.

A night on which I was compelled to commit a horrible act.

People that know me know me as a very happy, gracious fellow. A good, no great father. A good son and brother, a good neighbor. A good relative to all my relations. I was good. And I really was and still am by the grace of God. I was never overly angry, vengeful or mean spirited. In many ways I was most accommodating, easy going and helpful so my personality was certainly not one of barbaric hatred. But this night all was forsaken and I was about to become something else.

My marriage had fallen apart and on this night my wife had reveled to me some very unsettling truths. Weeks of trepidation, worry and consternation about our future and the future of our family finally came crashing in on me. Weeks and weeks of depression and stress pushed me beyond my limits of coping. Everything I knew about my life suddenly became unmade. Everything I believed was undone. A decade of truth became a lie. Prior to this night just going about my daily life was scarcely imaginable. The robotics of the work day was the only thing between me and my life coming to a complete halt. It is a feeling I am sure many others have encountered while progressing through similar situations. For me it was nothing short of total desperation as I tried to keep my children's lives functioning on some level and show up for work every day and actually do something other than cry or stare at the wall.

But this night was ground zero. The grand ignition and the flash. The news was confirmation of a broken heart and no hope to be seen on the horizon. It was over and here are the reasons.

At first it was unbelieving. This can't be, how is this possible? I know you. This just doesn't make sense. What about all the years, the kids, the history. In the end it all boiled down to useless snippets of conversation that meant nothing. Then anger took over. I cracked the top of a wooden cedar chest with my fist. I stomped and swore and made a general calamity, all while the children slept above us unaware that their life was about to derail when they woke from their happy dreams. To even recall that moment still brings me pain, 25 years later.

How could this happen to a loyal husband, dutiful father, a good Christian family man? God had abandoned my family. God was a traitor. God was a false god. An Idol. As mentioned in previous chapters, I suddenly became convinced that God wasn't even real. An instantaneous revelation of the folly in placing my trust in a myth. Praying to Horus was a more reasonable option.

I jumped up and down and finally stormed out of the bedroom. And then back in again and back out and then back in. She walked out into the living and sat on the couch as I slammed the bedroom door one final time.

It was late, I was tired, wired, strung out, wild eyed and everything else that comes when a wrathful hormone takes over your body. The only thing I could do was to sprawl across the bed and shake. I hated everyone and everything except my children. God was ruse. He was at the top of the list, higher up the hate ladder than my wife. If he existed I hated him. If he didn't, I hated the idea of his falsified creation and anyone who promulgated his name.

Emptiness and despair was all that was left behind. And yet I never did lose my own sense of being. I felt every stab of the loss in my heart. It was personal and real and human. Very human. The pain of a living breathing soul coming apart at the seams. I lay on the bed looking up at the ceiling not know what to do next. Hours passed and house was still. My wife had stretched out on the couch and fallen asleep. But for me there was no sleep. There was only the hollow, fearful agitation in the middle of my stomach, rolling and rolling itself over like the tumble of the clothes dryer. Anger began to rise up again and I wanted to just get up and smash another piece of furniture, when suddenly something changed.

I stood up, looking towards the hallway that led to the living room where my wife slept. My mind began to race and I felt a jolt of energy throughout my body. I almost felt slightly light headed and I attributed this to an adrenaline rush and then getting up quickly. But it didn't feel quite that way. It was as if something came up through me, like static electricity rising up from the floor. My thoughts got narrowed and darkened. Everything around me got blocked out. My mind was thrown down the hall and into the living room and it wanted revenged.

Thought came upon thought. Go finish her. She deserves it. Do it. One step, then two. But something set me to pause. Another thought pushed into my brain. Stop, what is this, this is not you,

you aren't like this. At once I became aware of not feeling in totally in control. I was a marionette, being moved about with purpose.

It was such a terrifying sensation that words seems to be inadequate to describe. I was not myself. Something had taken advantage of my mental state and had given me a push. There is no doubt that for a few moments, I became aware of something else with me.

And that awareness set me free. Evil cannot stand the light of truth; it hides in the shadows and masquerades inside your deepest fears. It whispers and suggests ideas when you are at your weakest. And yet the simplest action can defeat it. I was aware of this, thing and I acknowledged its presence. And at the moment I took a direct action it disengaged. Suddenly I was myself again, my own conscious being. I fell back onto the bed shaking hysterically, not only because of the action that I might have committed but also from the encounter.

Humans don't realize how perfectly easy they are to be compromised. No one senses their precarious animal character until they get a bad cold or the flu or something much worse like cancer. Suddenly your body is this flimsy shell trying to hold back an onslaught from nature's beasties.

Your spirit can suffer the same fate. It is constantly under assault, a never ending barrage of ungodliness that manifests from all directions of this cracked earthy realm of ours. TV, radio, social media, entertainment, books, games, preachers, poets, priests and even an occasional Pope or two can manifest it. Nothing and no one is outside the arena for potential corruption. The greatest and holiest of saints were constantly on guard, praying and fighting off their attacks. The Holy Mother Church itself was founded on the bones of one of the greatest traitors in history. But in Peter's story also lay the greatest hope to us all against our own battle with evil. It is a battle that we can win, but it is a war that must be fought for the rest of our mortal lives. The adversary will never stop, will never rest and will never yield his assaults until the day our soul is finally out of his reach.

I was suffering from a weakened mind, a weakened psyche and a weakened soul. I was trampled underfoot and ground into the family room carpeting. I was tired and scared.

And because of this condition, people would conclude that my perception of this horrid event is tainted by my mental state and is nothing more than the result of stress. The story of 'the devil made me do it' is just that, a story that every wild man could use as an excuse to commit his atrocities. Blame someone or something else for your actions. That may be true in some cases.

And to this end I would say, I would agree with that assessment, if it didn't happen to me. From the outside looking in, that's the plausible explanation for anyone having those sensations. That is exactly what one would expect as the diagnosis from the secular world. Demons are not real; they are only crutches to be used in a court case defense to prove innocence by insanity.

But the moment it happened, I knew something was different. I could feel, actually feel myself being invaded, violated, something. I can't even find the words to describe how it felt and I'm a writer, but you just can't translate the experience into words and accurately relate the event. These occurrences defy a communicated description. I only know this, one moment I was a sad, angry heartbroken man and then the next, I was something else. It was like knowing that you're dreaming while inside a dream but not being able to do anything about it.

Over the years I've spoken with many other individuals about my trials, such as various priests, counselors, friends and people I've met at retreats or other religious occasions. And I am not alone in these experiences. Not by a long shot. Many of them asked me if I felt that I was under some sort of a possession. Usually the answer is no, since, I don't have any idea what an actual bona fide, bring in the exorcist type possession feels like, so how would I know. My laypersons brain sees it much simpler. An entity, a bad bit of energy, an unnamed malevolence, a wisp of bad juju, a shadow from another dominion or a strange phenomenon shared my space for a brief moment and influenced my thoughts. They were already dark. It made them darker, much darker. Darkness right to the edge of humanity. It reached inside me as easily as an ocean breeze blows across loose sun baked sand.

The only thing that pulled me back was my own conscious studious awareness of other similar instances which I had come across in my reading over the years. And, just possibly a nudge from my own spiritual protector or protectors was involved as well. In fact I'm convinced there was a bit of divine intervention.

To the non-Catholic, such conversation in things like the awareness of demons all around us and angelic or sainted spirits coming for to our intervention must sound very odd indeed. That's understandable. To the Catholic, at least to the practicing Catholic who appreciates the entire collective of the faith, none of that sounds odd at all. In fact, it's downright ordinary, something we understood since childhood.

> Angel of God, my guardian dear
> to whom God's love commits me here.
> ever this day be at my side
> to light and guard, to rule and guide. Amen

Shame overwhelms me when I recall this moment. To be yourself one moment and then again not yourself is almost incomprehensible. I was unmade, a monster, a creature of a creature. It was the snap of knowing the absolute truth of the reality of evil. Not human evil, but non-human evil. Oh my god, this is real? They really exist, and I am that vulnerable? It was like I was living my whole life on a movie set and thinking the façade was the real world when in truth, everything observed was only window dressing held together by chicken wire. Then suddenly it all fell down leaving me shattered and terrified.

This event has never been relayed to anyone. I've never told it nor spoken about it since it happened. Why I relate it now in written form I can't say exactly.

One would think it an important sign post along the road towards finding oneself, recovering faith and setting on a path in the wake of such personal upheaval. I knew that the spiritual world was really-really real. I knew the bad side was out there trying to acquire souls through trickery and deception and by fomenting discourse. I knew it, positively.

And this did have a grave effect on me. Years after this event I projected myself into all the right places, I read all the right stuff, I said all the right prayers and put on the breastplate of God. I charged forward into friendly apologetics and religious internet chat forms. I did the retreat circuit, attended rosary prayer services, took bible study courses, taught Sunday school. You name it I did it. Sunday mass, weekday mass, Latin rite mass, Melkite mass, the longer the mass the better. I was invincible, indomitable and formidable; and brimming with false assumptions. I was arrogant.

Most arrogant religious zealots have no clue of what's actually happening all around them. They only know books, words. They argue in endless riddles for no other reason but to convince someone else that they are right about some biblical meaning turned in a phrase written in Greek. More blind guides one upon the other, tools to be used by the enemy.

Paper and leather cannot replace the actual experience that comes from an encounter with the very substance that all those words are trying to explain. The puffed up pride of the righteous know-it-all only helps to obscure the fact, not clarify it. Whether you use the Vulgate or the earliest Greek text to try to correlate the New Revised Edition phraseology with an Aramaic maxim means absolutely nothing if you can't see the point behind it all. In the end, if you miss the point, none of that matters.

But it matters to the enemy. Fracturing the word of God is a weapon. People that dwell and thrive on taking apart the holy words and then putting them back together as they see fit can become a weapon to be wielded by the army of the darkness.

These adversaries are real. They are not just concepts, words or ideas. They live outside of the page, outside time and space.

This does not mean striving to understand the word of God is bad. This does not mean that teaching or clarifying the word of God is bad. This does not mean that having a particular view into the meaning of the word of God is bad. But the obsessive adoration of the alphabetic arrangement of the word to the point of blindness is not only bad but dangerous. You cease to engage in the spirit and become a slave of the page. You construct walls and compile lists of your religious opponents whom you must defeat and destroy with your brilliance and depth of understanding, all while the real enemy, whom your zeal conceals, inflates your ego and whispers your praise.

We the clueless, mill about our daily activities completely oblivious of the evil that trails our every step. And every step I took along my path to self-righteousness was shadowed by an op-portunistic companion. It almost got me to slide once, while I was weak and standing in a dark bedroom, shaken and emotionally compromised. It almost pressed me into committing a heinous act. By the grace of God, I acknowledged its presence and walked away and so I drew off on a more *glorious* path . . . but it never left my side. It waited, off at a distance for another opportunity to have me stumble and fall to the edge of the void. Patiently, gleefully it watched as I reveled in a false confidence.

And it waited. Until I met her. Then it knew, now was the time for ideas, for whispers, for notions of lust, for a justification in my angry loneliness. It moved in closer until it was right alongside me. And I listened to its stories, about my grief and about what I deserved out of life, about my loss and who was to blame. It was easy, so easy. All my false convictions melted away like butter and I was left naked, both in spirit and in the flesh, crawling around a cheap room in an room along the interstate.

✳

Looking back on that night makes me quiver with disgust. How far can a soul go, be pushed. I always worried about her husband finding out and him being pushed to the brink, as I once was, into taking a drastic action. We would talk about that possibility now and then; and uncomfortable conversation indeed. Thinking about the scandal that would be left in the wake, my image being torn asunder before the eyes of my children had always haunted me. Not enough to keep my pants on but enough to give me some bit of pause before undoing my belt buckle.

X

SYMBOLUM

THE TENTH STATION: JESUS is stripped of his garments: We adore you O Christ and we praise you, for by your holy cross you have redeemed the world.

Even naked, Jesus clearly exhibited the mark of his creed. With every whip and chain and every pierce of his flesh he wore the sign. How many bits of skin were torn away on my account? Some of my Protestant friends would say that in the end it doesn't matter; all that mattered was that he died. But I saw the wounds. They encircled his body as the snake from the Garden giving him one last squeeze.

Christians have a mark, one given at baptism that flays both body and soul. But it is also human nature to want to bear a mark openly and proudly. It can be a priest choking in a Roman collar or a Evangelical minister pacing the stage with his fingers clutching his worn out bible until it bleeds.

I trotted out my markings openly and proudly as well. Stickers on my car window that said 'Keep Christ in Christmas' and 'RC', chains around my neck with medals of Blessed Mary and the Saints, crucifixes strategically placed all around the house, pictures of angels, religious calendars, emblems, signs and symbols in abundance. They all had true meaning to me and in my heart

I embraced every bit of what they suggested. That I loved God, I loved his Church and I loved his emissaries in all forms. The grand contradiction.

And symbols *are* worthy and useful. They are reminders, billboards and rallying points. They can give us comfort or become a bit of conscience.

But people can drive through red lights and stop signs, exceed the speed limit and take two free mints even when the sign says one per customer. Society is flawed. We constantly need reminders. Which is why the priest chaffs at his Roman collar but wears it none the less or the vicar digs his fingernails deep into his favorite bible as he swings it to and fro. Grasping that bible is like holding a lifeline to God. He dare not let it go.

Sometimes letting go can happen in steps and stages and sometimes all at once. Sometimes you are aware and sometimes you never knew it even happened. I let go, not all at once but in stages. As my animal instinct began to override my intellect, the sacred words and holy symbols lost their power over me as I gave myself over to the power of the enemy.

The woman in my life became the main driver. The crucifixes and prayer cards still hung in their place but I no longer noticed them. Whenever I would meet her, I would remove my 'Our Lady of the Miraculous Medal' chain. As I was removing my pants, I would stuff Mary into my pants pocket so she wouldn't be able to witness me committing infidelity. It was an exercise in mental gymnastics, my guilt wrestling with my lust.

I was a pig not a man. Rooting in the dirt for love and sex and pretending to be ordinary on some level but just enough yearning to keep me from believing truth of the gospel.

All in or all out. Either accept Christ's salvific act, or don't. Acting the normal life is only just that, acting. Mary's eyes were not blinded by the cotton lining inside my pants pocket. Every time the curtains closed and sheets became unmade, my soul was laid bare to the heavens and all the rationalized gamesmanship and all the sacred markers couldn't change that.

And it went on and on; on for years, for a decade and more. Time came and went and the outward signs remained but the internal fakery began to take its toll. Every time I removed my medal and shoved Mary into my pants pocket a little bit more of my soul passed away. I could feel it, ebbing. It was the deal I struck without being aware of the terms on the contract. Not in the sense that I made a pact with the devil, like Faust, but more of an unspoken understanding.

On one hand I was a model Christian and on the other a model pagan. I lived in duality, both halves aware, in conjunction and with cooperation. The bad side put up with my religiosity out of necessity. The good side accepted my lustful weakness out of pity. And the deeper I went into sin the larger my appearance of orthodoxy became. The one who proclaims their innocence the loudest is usually guilty. That became my pattern.

It was a total mess, an amorphous pile of crap and I rolled with it. And if anyone doubts the power of genetically driven sexuality, turbo charged by an unholy spirit, then remember this . . .

I DISCERNED that I had two, not one, but two actual, first person, recognizable, lucid, tangible, relatable, startling, in the flesh encounters with spirits from outside time and space, from beyond our realm of comprehension. First, on one dark and lonely night when I was almost driven mad and second, in church when the Holy Spirit or God or whatever it was manifested a clear message inside my consciousness. Twice I had encounters, twice.

People who don't know me may automatically assume I'm some sort of hysterical nut who sees the face of Jesus in a piece of burnt toast or an oil slick or speaks in tongues on any given Sunday or is routinely medicated to control some form of religious hysteria. None of that is true.

The fact is I've handled plenty of adversity very-very well. Outside of the few large bumps, life had been totally regular, routine and steady and my daily life became settled and organized.

And so it was when I met her, not long after the divorce had finally sorted itself out. My life was very much back on track.

But even after having *two* close encounters of an unknown kind, I STILL could not resist my masculine programming regardless of any grave sin committed in the process. Not even definitive proof in the reality of an alt-world could stop me from a hot dogging rendezvous in some empty parking lot. People like to joke about spiritual evidence, the proof they need before believing. For some, Jesus would have to come down upon demand into the middle of a packed football stadium and show his bloody wounds to the howling mob before they'd believe, or God the first person would have to answer a dare spelled out on the front page of the New York Times and make it snow at the equator in July. Then and only then, would they believe and anything other than the tangible spectacular showing are just fairy tales and ghost stories told to children and gullible imbecils by old women from oddly named countries. Tales from the old country. Spooks and ghosts. God and his many assorted magical characters.

My terms for belief were far less challenging. And they were answered. And I believed, in total and in complete fidelity to the faith. And I still went astray. I KNEW this was from God and I still betrayed him. I was Judas, I was Peter, I was weak and I ran.

If I was at that football stadium when Jesus descended to the mob, I would have howled loudly at his wounds and fell to my knees on the peanut strewn floor with the rest of them. "Look, my fellow doubter, finally, the great sign hath cometh! To see it with my own eyes, the privileged masses, the chosen to be at this blessed arena. All praise and glory be the name of Jesus, halleluiah! Oh and hey, can we get a beer over here please?" And after it was all over, and the euphoria floated away, I'd drive off to the dirty motel and knock on the dirty door. "Knock-knock, guess who, you won't believe what just happened to me at the game."

Symbols and signs are only as good as the person reading them. Once I was a witness and understood. Then the meaning disappeared, obscured by sin. The form remained but the element was gone.

God reached out to me from different directions. Even the actions of the devil were allowed by Gods A scare, a warning. Slow down, sharp curve ahead.

Nothing could slow me down in my race to the edge of the road. She'd reach out and I'd respond. I'd reach out and she'd respond. The dance went on.

Realization that I was following my own father's footsteps didn't sway me from the path. He was a common philanderer. I was in love and only cheating with one woman, my steady partner. It was a true relationship and not some sordid one night stand or a series of conquests. Behavior once hated during an unsettled childhood now became dust to be swept under the rug. Everything despised in my father's actions apparently had no correlation to any actions taken on my part. Disconnected and unrelated, the brain reorganizing truth to suit the occasion, like so many politicians in Washington bending facts to better fit the narrative. Words become the tool and the means to get what you want. There is always a better way of telling a lie, until even you believe it.

Now it all seems obvious, so utterly ridiculous that my actions completely mirrored my father, maybe not in method but in aim. And he was surely poked and prodded by his own demons following him around were ever he went, whispering opportunities and reminding him of what he deserved from life. Could the same demon infect father and son, timeless beings just waiting for another crack at a family member or two? Why not, they are not bound by the passing of the decades. Doubtless my evil companion attached itself to thousands, maybe tens of thousands over the course of humankind. Creations from the foundation of creation afterward employed to harass and pester, to cajole and deceived for the millenniums. "Hey, agent 66, didn't you work over the old man? His kid is ready for a good push; go give him a swift kick in the butt." Like ol' Screwtape, barking out orders and sending his legions out to war.

In the movies, evil usually has a face and you can usually see it coming. And the hero is equipped with the symbols of opposition. Crucifixes, bibles, garments, holy water. And in some cases that still holds accurate for the real world, that evil can be such an overriding and powerful force that the cavalry needs to be brought in. It is real and those steps necessary. But the majority of the world suffers in the darkness that comes from obliviousness. Typically there is no face to an evil other than what appears in your bathroom mirror. True darkness is hidden and cloaked by daily living. It is buried under science and math and politic and it slinks beneath our general apathy towards anything that constricts our desires. Whatever is hindering us from commenting sin it attacks. All the pointed towers we build with crosses raised toward heaven cannot counter the depth to which we plunge.

She wore a cross. Golden and shining. Lovely to look at and she wore it proudly. Everything the cross stood for she believed. It wasn't just a vain symbol, just some vanity to be worn to show people that she was better than they were because she had a faith that was worthy of carrying the mark. She loved God. Her parents loved God, very strongly. And yet she erred. We all can and may have.

If Gods own handmade creation in Adam can falter, if Cain can become a murderer, if Abraham can lie, if David can betray his oath, if the Apostles can reject their best friend at his darkest hour, then who are we? Are we less vulnerable than the Patriarchs and the founders of Christianity? Anyone who assumes their own invincibility is already compromised. We should strive to put on the armor of the Lord because we are in a fight and not because it makes unassailable.

I knowingly, willingly stripped away my armor. It was unceremoniously dumped for a good time, for a romp, a year after year after year fling of a thing. Oh the happiness and the joy it stirred in hell to see me play the polymath. Joyfulness tinged with hatred.

Sexual desire is a powerful flaw. It seems a great flaw in our construction to include such a weak link, a great hindrance towards aspirations of immortality. Such are us creatures made of dirt thereafter to be condemned to spend our mortal days playing in the mud. It's really not fair. The tug of war started with the opposition having a lot more rope before the whistle even blew. Was this intended by our creator, to give us struggle and will and to give the adversary an advantage? For what purpose?

An average man like me had found it incomprehensible to define any rational explanation for God burdening me with such an exploitable impediment. All manner of deep thinkers, theologians, philosophers, pious zealots and religious crack pots have come up with explanations for our vulnerable state, none of which I can agree with nor completely understand.

I only know that it's true. All the Doctors of the Church, Fathers of the Church, all the Popes and the Cardinals, all the doctors of theology from the myriad of universities, the book writers, the talk show hosts, late night televangelists, none of them can fully explain why Satan was given such an easy time over us. I only know that it's true.

Many have trodden the same path. The number of people who have fallen into unholy relationships is as numerous as the stars in the heavens. In our time the iniquity grinds ever forward, in constant motion since the days before the great deluge wiped the slate clean, only to start moving again once the waters receded. I was never alone in my quest for damnation. I was surrounded by a fellowship of the damned.

※

Once, I lost my 'Our Lady of the Miraculous Medal' medal. I searched everywhere for it. To my mind, Mary had finally had enough and took her leave from me. Like Gollum's ring, the medal abandoned me. I really believed this, I truly did. This was a sign; she was done hiding in my pants pocket. Frantically searching yielded no results. It had to be in the house somewhere and all the likely spots were gleaned over. Nothing. Guilt flooded me, as clearly my antics ultimately pushed her away. The symbology of losing a symbol did what it was intended to do, to point out, to remind, to cause an effect. Even in sin I clung to God like a man afraid to let go of a life raft. A piece of me needed to feel the possibility of redemption was always available when I was ready to accept it. My Protestant friends said it mattered not, since Jesus died once and for all and your personal relationship has saved you, regardless of what you do after. This creed, this belief to me felt so wrong on so many levels. I knew I was living outside of God, outside of his laws, separated and apart by choice. My actions mattered, they had consequences, I could feel it, feel my soul rotting away, the grace of God being rejected by my intellect like a bad germ. Anyone who denies their actions and uses the blood of Christ as an excuse to do their own will is deluding themselves. It is once again a corruption by mankind's wanton desire which allows us to be swindled into believing we can do no wrong as long as we kept Jesus in our heart while doing it.

One day, after many weeks of searching I gave up. I felt repentant, in the truest form. I had told my lady friend that we needed to 'take a break'. This didn't go over very well, but my course was set. My mind relaxed as it pulled out of the relationship and a gentle peace came over me.

The next morning I opened a dresser drawer that held all form of miscellaneous items such as hair brushes, watches, loose change, rings and the like.

There was my medal. Had it gotten shuffled under some of those other items and then with the pulling action of opening the drawer, it possibly came loose from the pile of rubble? I had searched that drawer over and over and over with no results.

I put the medal around my neck and felt a sense of relief. It was back and I was whole again. There is no understanding in these actions. Only pity.

XI

FIRST CONFESSION

THOSE FIRST FEW YEARS after my divorce became a time of many graces. There was never period in my life that I was ever closer to the lord than during the post breakup, prior to the affair. It was a time of immense growth and self-awareness. Counseling, both spiritual and professional helped balance the inner turmoil. Things were finally put right. God called out to me and I answered. The beatific voice spoke and a door to another world swung wide open. For the first time, all had been revealed, the good and the bad. The devil stands very close to God and if you get close enough, you will encounter them mutually.

But that is a validation beyond all human certainty. When the demon comes to torment your dreams and mock your faith, rejoice, for you are standing very close to the ultimate revelation. And that revelation, that God is a reality, makes all else superfluous. Every doubt you ever supposed or thought has now been definitively answered.

I shared that experience. I believed and saw the light, and the demon came for me. And in the beginning I was strong. And as I was mocked, so I mocked in return. Having foreknowledge of those attacks and in what manner they would come made it easier to recognize and cast off any assault by the adversary.

Long conversions would subsequently be held between myself and other fellow sufferers and we would chuckle and sniffle over each other's stories. "Ok, hey there, mister devil, I know it's really you hiding in that TV commercial, I found you out, so just move along, it's not gonna work this time." The answerer of an individual who was overflowing with certainty.

Ah, but mankind has known such certainty before and still rebelled under its own willfulness; in the first Garden, at the base of Mount Sinai. I was a much lesser man than the one created from Gods own hand, as was Adam and yet he fell.

But for a time I shone with the sun of righteousness and all was goodness and glory. There were no particular temptations that were overpowering or unmanageable and my faith soared.

Then she came to me. At that time the dating scene wasn't particularly successful or appealing either. Loneliness began to grow and eventually it became a powerful weapon that was used against me. Gods' spirit could not substitute for the touch of another human. Simply craving the warmth of another pushed me along a path that ultimately led to sin and ruination.

Years of hiding, sneaking and slinking about ensued and we reveled in our affair. I enjoyed her company so much that any notion of the occasion of sin became incomprehensible and I rationalized the relationship in one way or another until it fit my need.

Then, one day my oldest daughter started asking questions. She saw the texts, the phone calls. Who was this woman, a friend, a girlfriend, why didn't she ever come around? She was never around for holidays or special occasions, a mystery woman. My answers were varied and thin, lies on top of lies, which spread in all directions like tendrils.

Thought turned into contemplation which gradually turned into guilt. So much guilt; Catholic guilt, fatherly guilt. If put on trial the verdict was clearly guilty. What sort of image would this put upon me if anyone found out? The family scandal, forever laying waste to my memory and destroying all the well-meant morality that I imparted onto my children. Washed away in an instant by a blinding desire to take another man's wife to bed.

Of all the menacing dangers and opportunities for tragedy, this nuclear family development actually got through to me. Not that it had an immediate impact on my actions. The fun and games continued onward and upward on a straight trajectory into outer space. But the seeds were planted. Oh the shame, the bitter anguish the children would have to endure because their father was a liar and a cheat and not who they were duped into believing by all his moralistic prattle.

What was the real character inside the father figure? Even I wasn't sure anymore. All around good guy and a faithful servant of God, a great provider who was good with tools, always the helpful and generous neighbor ready with a quick smile? Or was it the hidden lonely soul, unsure in life? Possibly nothing more than a lustful animal and a sexually voracious liar; the embodiment of the consummate sinner.

It didn't take a college degree to see the mess I'd become. A tangled up, mangled up collection of clashing neurons that fought in that grand war that was my intellect. On one side was every-thing that made me a wonderful person and they were varied and voluminous. And on the other side was my sexual lust along with other dotted components of human faults. But with that one mag-nificent lustful vice on their front line, it was no contest. An army of virtues could not defeat this one foe. A vice so powerful that everything good about me could be undone in an instant, as if none of it ever existed.

After I met her, all that I was before changed. God came and went in my life like dandruff, more of an annoyance than a heal-ing. I was turned inside out and outside in. Any progress after the divorce to more a righteous life made a sudden left turn straight towards hell. And I reveled in the brimstone, for a few years. But my conscience played tricks on me. It would not leave me alone in my dissolution. Like a specter it hovered about, prodding and reprimanding, taking shots at my actions from hither and yon.

Guilt and cross-examination flared up in-between the mid-night back seat romps and bathroom funsy feel-ups. Then a chance encounter with a very holy priest momentarily wrestled me back from the clutches of my sexual mania.

The duality of my life at that time fortunately always kept one of my toes stuck firmly into the life of prayer. To be rooted in spirit and yet carnally physical was maddening but that one toe, hanging onto that piece of residual holiness still inside me got me back to the basilica where I had heard 'the voice' inside my head. Even in my debauchery, the pretense of caring about my Catholic heritage would guide me back into old learned ritualist practices..

These practices would temporarily straighten out my path. The standard application of saying a Hail Mary or an Angelus was like learning to ride a bike. It came back naturally from somewhere deep within the stored programming. It kept a part of me sane. It kept a part of me aware. It kept part of me alive.

One day during a lunch break, I rode over to the great basilica. This was something I would do at least a few times a month. The silence and chill of the vast main structure was so appealing on a hot summer day that it could wring out a meditative daydream. I would sit there and drift about with no thought on any particular subject coming into my head, which in itself was amazing as my thought processing never stops. Except in there. Which is why I gathered, that I was open to feeling 'the voice' inside my head that one great and terrible day.

This day, I just sat, drifting, floating, eyes closed, thinking about nothing, when I heard a voice once again. This time it came from alongside me. My eyes darted open and standing in the aisle was a middle-age Passionist priest wearing his long black garment with a heart and cross symbol on it which read 'Jesu Xpi Passio', which translates into Jesus Christ Passion.

The order was founded by Saint Paul of the Cross and his statue is in a place of honor in the lower level. There was no one else in the church yet I didn't hear him approach.

"I didn't mean to startle you," he said in a low voice, "but I saw you here a few weeks ago, in line for confession as I was walking around the back, but you left before you got to go in."

"Yes, I replied, I had to get back to work, I was running late," which was a lie. Actually I had decided at that moment that I did NOT want to give up my lustful life and turned away from confession at the last second.

"I saw you again," he continued, "and just figured I'd ask if there was anything you wanted to talk about."

Bang. Doom. The dark clouds began to close in about me. I could feel my throat tighten and my stomach acid churning and roiling like molten steel in a caldron. I was trapped in that pew like a rat. Time began to move slower and slower. What would I say, how would I answer.

My life was so twisted up that even I wasn't exactly sure what was going to come out of my mouth at any given time. When it came to lying and the sinful ways, I never knew what I was going to say or why I would say it.

"No Father, I'm good, I was just sitting here meditating before going back to work. But thank you for asking, really, that was very thoughtful."

Thoughtful . . . it was thoughtful? It was more than thoughtful, it was insightful, it was inspired, he knew. He could smell this rat a mile away. He saw me dodge out the door that day and he could tell I was on the run. Then by fate or with the guidance of some other unseen force he chances into me again, alone.

Coincidences of this variety happened to me time after time after time. It seemed that this willful priest wasn't afraid to catch people off guard and back them into situation where a decision had to be made. Here is your chance, take or leave it. I left it.

"Ok, well, have a nice afternoon and I hope to see you here again." And with that, he proceeded to shuffle off down the aisle heading towards the large oak exit door to the left of the grand altar.

"Wait, Father, since you're here, I may as well have a chat if you have a minute," the words coming out surprisingly. He sat back down, his facial expression not changing in the least.

"What's up?" he said softly.

"Quite a bit actually, now that you're asking. For one, I'm, a . . . an adulterer, amongst other things."

"Really, you don't look the part, but I suppose no one does, on the outside at least," he replied with a very slight smirk.

"Well I am, trust me on that," I said with a larger smirk, "and not very proud to hear those words come out of my mouth."

"Then why don't you stop doing it?"

"I don't want to stop."

"Then what's there to chat about?"

"Because I know I need to stop, and . . . I need a good reason."

"You're expecting me to give you a good reason to not go to hell, well, I am a priest so I guess I can understand why you'd expect something like that, but that's not how it works. God made up the rules and I can only help you remember it. You're fate, that's the only reason you need to stop. What more of a reason can there be. Every consequence from your adultery leads to the same result and it's that result which should be your reason to stop."

"What result is that?" I aksed.

"Separation and Desolation. Big words, spooky words. We live our tiny lives day to day. Right now you can only see your physical desire so for you, tomorrow is another day, and you can worry on your sins tomorrow, but tomorrow may never come. There are some things that are worth worrying about every day of your life and the fate of your soul is number one. How am I doing?"

"It's a difficult thing to deal with, desire, in fact it feels nearly impossible to overcome at times."

"I'm a priest, remember, we have our own problems as I'm sure you're aware, a lot more than we should but none the less, no one is immune to biology. It's the test of the will and unfortunately the flesh is weak, right, like you don't know that. But, that's why the Lord opened the door to forgiveness. Because we are all like Peter, weak men who need a hand to turn back from the darkness. I always liked that expression; I read that in a sermon once."

"I do feel guilt, lately I mean, most of the time I can't stand myself. I think about how my children would react if they found out, what people would think. I never used to care but that's changed."

"Well, that's good, but this more about you personally than what other people would think of you. You're more worried about being found out and everyone thinking you're a bad guy than your own fate. That's the blindness of the mortal world and the devil. He tries to keep you busy and disconnected from what he has in store for you." He smiled when he said this and it gave me a bit of a shiver because it felt spiritually sinister.

"Ok, well, then, maybe I can make a confession and hope it sticks this time."

"I don't think I've ever heard anyone say that before, that's a new one. All that matters is that you mean it; want to repent and you want God to forgive you. Right now. And when the temptation comes around again, well, all we can ask for is the grace to be strong and resist. And that little bit of Catholic guilt doesn't hurt you either."

I said what was needed to be said and he said what was needed to be said. In the end he gave me absolution and few bits of penance which included my few mea culpas but more importantly, a spiritual exercise in the form of the Saint Michaels Prayer. It was this priest, the man in the long black cassock who was the first to actually teach me what it meant. In the past I would just blurt out the rehearsed lines. The long-standing confrontational prayer to the demonic world crafted by Pope Leo XIII after a vision he had of Satan boasting over the destruction of the Church and God allowing him enough time to attempt his futile plan. The Pope also saw the armies of the devil gathering around the Rome and preparing for an attack; an attack I would venture to say was somewhat successful on various levels.

But not totally, the attack would never be totally successful. And it was and still is a very powerful prayer. Of course prayer is only a collection of words and words have no power in and of themselves. It is the spiritual intent behind those words that have the power and the words give that intent its focus and direction.

When the Lord bid us to pray, 'deliver us from evil', it is our intent by his instruction that gives that prayer strength. The Pope implored the help of an Archangel, a creation that since all eternity began stood in the presence of God. And the Pope new exactly what his intent was.

'Saint Michael the Archangel, defend us in battle, be our
protection against the wickedness
and snares of the devil. May God rebuke him we humbly pray; and do thou,
O Prince of the Heavenly host, by the power of God,
cast into hell Satan and all the evil spirits who prowl
about the world seeking the ruin of souls. Amen'

This shortened English translation is the most widely used and the version given to me that day. My spiritual exercise and training was to recite this poem out loud every time 'the urge' came upon me. Whenever the Devil reached into my loins to fan my wantonness, I was to rebuke him with forceful word. Not only would this be a defensive measure, reminding myself verbally of my unwise impending action but also as an offensive measure. I was sending out the heavenly host before me, them standing toe to toe with the fork tailed eternal abomination and his cohorts. 'Advance no further, dare not cross this line, we rebuke thee!' Or something like that.

This whole thing sounded like poppycock. How much 'power' a bunch of words had over the spiritual realm wasn't really clear to me. What was clear, was that this priest believed they did. His gaze tore straight through me when he read the holy words and gave me his simple instructions. He was adamant and direct and assured in this belief. One tiny piece of laminated paper could send demons in flight, biblical in its very nature.

Not an hour would go by that I would not need to recite that prayer. My passions were constantly inflamed. Not that I was some sort of sex addict or lecherous fiend but every average male had some carnal idea flash though his mind on and off throughout the day.

See a woman with a tight sweater or a smooth leg or a pretty neck line and the programming would kick in. Before you even realized it you would be thinking of all manner of lurid situations. To even think such things could be considered a sin.

But how could one avoid the dot and dash of the jangling computer inside your skull? If just picturing these acts inside that skull was a sin, then what was the consequence of actually doing it? Was there anything beyond sin? If so, I had it. Because throughout the day, I wrestled with the thought of my sexual encounters, the magnitude of the pleasure we both experienced and it kept me wanting more. How could some crazy words written by a dead Pope, one hundred and forty years ago stop any of that?

Conveniently the one item in this equation purposely ignored and overlooked was free will. And free will can be trained. Awareness can be ignited. Programming can be altered or sub routines added. We are only slaves to our basic programming if we allow it. The pretense that I was only doing what nature engrained in me was a lie. Nature only dictates that I procreate, not have sex in closets with another man's wife. All the additional encoding was added by me, not by biology. And I could de-program . . . if I wanted to. Somehow, this spiritual training and little prayer card was supposed to help me do just that.

On his way out the priest stopped at the exit door and faced the grand alter and knelt down, blessed himself and then stood up gazing intently at the large cross and corpus that hung over the back wall. It seemed as if time stopped. His eyes never left the scene, as if he was in a trance or some other meditative state. Then he turned back to me and said, 'just do it,' and then quietly withdrew.

I put the prayer card in my pocket not knowing exactly what I was going to do with it; possibly use it as a book marker in my old bible or just file in a dresser drawer with some old funeral cards.

It went into the bible at Isaiah 53, the Suffering Servant passage, which I usually read during Lent as part of my Lenten observance.

I was the white washed tomb, all spotless on the outside but on the inside, all spiritual desolation and moral corruption.

The church was so quite that the sound of my breathing caused a slight echo and the faint scent of wax burning one floor below wafted up along the rear staircase and into the nave. Standing and walking slowly to the rear door, an old man came in moving very slowly. He looked up and smiled.

"It's a good day when I can still get myself here," he said.

"Yes, that's always a good day," I replied.

"Hope you got what you came looking for," he said in return and strolled over to the closest pew and took a seat. Then he pulled out a worn out prayer booklet.

That was a very odd thing for him to say given the recent priestly encounter but then again maybe not. It was a church after all and people could assume the reason you would be there by yourself on a warm midafternoon was to pray for some personal need or another. The basilica was known for attracting people in need.

Turning away from the old man, the smell of the wax could not be ignored. The lower basilica candle room was ablaze in color; the blue, red, green and purple dancing from the inner flame. I loved the smell of the candles. It smelled of a childhood memory and of holy days and of holidays.

Pulling the long stick out of the can of sand was a ritual that grounded my mind in a time when I was a better person and recollecting walking with my grandmother to the candle rack inside our predominately Italian-American parish and lighting one in honor of her mother.

Deep under the basilica was that cosy refuge of wax and heat, old long burnt incense, hard oak pews and the beautiful statue of the saint bedecked in flowers. And all was silence and peace.

I put four quarters into to offertory and lit a red glass candle. The pew squeaked and croaked under my weight. For some reason the idea of reading the prayer card came out of nowhere. It rolled along, every word now sounding as if that priest was still there reciting it back, his voice imprinted into the rhyme. Saint Michael the Archangel, defend us in battle, Saint Michael the Archangel, defend us in battle, Saint Michael the Archangel and on it went, reading it over and over. I could hear his intonation; Rebuke him we humbly pray, REBUKE HIM we humbly pray, over and over.

The card went back into the pocket. A strange calmness was upon me, much more than usual. The candle room always put me at ease but this was different. Going up the well-worn limestone staircase and out into the daylight didn't decrease the feeling. Even sitting back at the job desk didn't seem to affect the feeling. After an hour of doing basically nothing productive, the gears began to click again and the work began to flow. Then my cell phone went off. It was her.

✳

A priest is not like the average human in all things. But he is like the average human in most things. All are human and are therefore flawed and breakable. They can be the most glorious of men or the most horrid of monsters. Being ordained does not exclude them from temptation. On the contrary, it puts a bullseye on their back. In all the four corners of this rotten world there is nothing the demons hate more than The Church and its representatives. If I, an insignificant piece of dust found myself tormented for just attempting to follow the truth, a spiritual leader would be even bigger prey. Pastors, ministers and priests, nuns and holy lay women. All targets. When an army is on the attack, the first thing the opposition is trained to do is to identify the officers and take them out. It is a good strategy to employ, even for the forces of Hell. By this priest passing along a prayer card to me as defensive weapon, he himself would pay a price for his action

XII

THE REFUGE OF SINNERS

I ANSWERED THE PHONE call. She was sweet and lovely as usual, always happy and positive regardless of the mess swirling around her. The lines of the prayer ran through my head but quickly they began to fade. I could feel any strength I gained from my priestly encounter eroding away and soon, images of naked breasts took their place in my mind. My demonic shadow wasted little time regaining any footing it had lost. Before the call ended the plans were laid.

What lust a man has within. There wasn't even a struggle. Rolling over was easy. The allure of sexual gratification and the need for passing companionship was much more authoritative than a piece of laminated paper. Obviously that priest was mistaken and totally devoid of any understanding of the non-clerical world, the real world.

The real world was full of vice. The real world was full of temptation. The real world was full of desire. Temptation and desire dovetailed together nicely, like the tightest joint of a Shaker built drawer. How was a placard with some long dead Pontiffs ramblings going to undo all of that?

In this case it did not. There was a time that I actually used this old prayer once before to chase away demons at the suggestion of my sister, back when my divorce was finalized and my spiritual zeal began to peak when I had the strange encounter with my computer searches turning up bizarre topics.

And it worked, even though I paid little attention to the actual words. But this time, to my fractured understanding, I wasn't really praying away demons, but praying away my affair and I still wasn't sure I wanted to do that. It's one thing to ask God to prevent the demons from persecuting you on your search for righteousness but something very different to ask God to prevent the demons from tempting you to do something you already wanted to do.

Or is it? A person mired in the sin of commission can think many a crazy thing. When you are totally 'onboard' with a bad idea it doesn't matter who the captain of the ship is, even if it's Charon ferrying you across the river Styx. You're along for the ride. And I was along for the ride.

My lover was my refuge. It was to her that I ran; for sex, for compassion, for understanding, for solace, for friendship, for advice, for sex.

But it wasn't without guilt. The pointed sermon still came now and then directed right at me or an off-hand cutting remark about adultery made by a family member. The slap in the face, God poking me in the ribs. Yet I trudged onward. I didn't run to God for forgiveness. Maybe I was a really a good Protestant after all. Jesus completed his mission and therefore I was freed of sin; and therefore enabled to continue to sin.

A good Born Again would say not so fast, since I didn't accept Jesus into my heart around a campfire meeting or at the local hall using the prescribed and acceptable words and hand motions. But that wasn't true, I had and I did accept Jesus as my Lord and Savior, in no uncertain terms and not only in my heart but in my mind and soul. And many people knew this to be true; I wasn't without witness of my confession of this fact.

But saying you accept something isn't enough. If you don't act Christ like, then your words are just words. You can accept a free gift. But you can always return it or throw it away.

Somehow the evangelical theory that God's grace of forgiveness that was taken up by Jesus on the cross, can never be lost once you 'accept him', even if you reject him with your deeds makes no sense to me. A few very dear friends of mine live their lives under this belief. Good strong evangelicals, born again under the strictest of formulas, who have indulged in grievous sin after grievous sin, without ever fully rejecting that sin, and yet, deeply believe that the gates of heaven will swing wide open when their time comes regardless of what they've done or are still doing, as long as they tithe their 10%. I wish I could have believed in such things. It would have made my life so much easier. Like an eschatological 'get out of jail free' game card. Here you go son, what's to worry, just show it at the door when you get there and in you go. Please admit one believer. Catholics have their magic prayers and the non-denominational have their percentages. We all gravitated to whatever gave us the most comfort it seemed.

Despite all my recalcitrant behavior, I was a true believer, which is the dichotomy of being me, an adulterous disciple of Christ. I was a paradox, even to myself.

And so the meet ups and feel ups would continue, twisting around every corner to get the most out of our time together. The lies and deceptions would continue. The risk taking would continue. The mental gymnastics would continue. The guilt and unguilt would continue.

More than once I would answer her call and no one would be on the other end. Was it her husband or just a dropped call?

A dropped call was most probable since her calls always came while driving. But the silence on the other end of the phone was always unsettling. It got to the point that when her call came through, I would pick up the call but not answer, waiting for her first 'hello'. She used a different service for our calls and texts, but that didn't stop me from being cautious about what I said on a text or what I did when answering her call. Games upon games; Russian roulette and a roll of the dice.

Why would anyone want to live like this? Hell enjoys a target living on the edge of reason. One shot and off you go. Living beyond reason is very easy thing to do, almost too easy. Find something you want to do bad enough and rational analytical thinking disengages and the monkey brain kicks in.

Basic and primitive, created either through Darwin's evolution of mankind or in the antediluvian patriarchal revolution in the Garden. Regardless of how it came about, the dust from whence we came never stopped leading us back to the rawness of the earth. Like bad wiring, always ready to overload and burn down the house.

I choose to live in a house with the circuit's sizzling. After a while I began to feel it was quite ordinary and normal. Only the occasional tingle of concern would add a sense of reality.

Underneath it all, regardless of how cavalier I acted or reacted to what I was doing, the guilt was always there. I wanted what I wanted and did what I wanted, switching off as many parts of the brain that would fight my desires along my path to damnation. But the spiritual conditioning acquired over the length of my lifetime, from childhood to present day, was never unattended by the Holy Spirit.

It dwelled inside me, buried, hardly alive, but alive none the less. The guilt never totally went away. It played upon me at opportune times and it waited for that one action that would set it free. And that action came in the form of a single sentence comprised of five words.

"I really respect you, dad," my oldest daughter started in with our conversation.

"OK, what brought that on?"

"I don't know, but you're so predictable, in a good way. We can count on you to be consistent I guess. What you see is what you get I mean. It's sort of comforting to know."

To say I was devastated was like saying finding life on Mars was no big deal. That word does not begin to describe the emotional crush that was upon me. My daughter felt comforted by a hoaxer, a charlatan, a two-faced doubled up liar perpetrating of facade on her and the rest of the family.

Respect me? Respect? If anyone was more undeserving of adulation than me seemed an impossibility. I was, in the immortal words of Jackie Gleason, *a* bum; a no good, talking out of both sides of my mouth, flimflamming snake in the grass bum. The only thing that I was predictable or consistent about was my unpredictability and inconsistency with the truth.

She looked at me and saw the look. It was a look of shame. My eyes began to soften with tears.

"Oh my god, I didn't mean to embarrass you, are you OK?" she said with a loving smile.

"Ha, ya, I'm fine," I replied trying to laugh it off to fatherly pride rather than shame.

Fatherly pride was a joke. It wasn't because she was so gratified by what sort of person I was and it touched me deeply to hear it. It wasn't because my daughter respected me so much that she felt compelled to tell me and I was proud of the job I did raising her. It wasn't because I felt honored to be her dad.

It was because I felt shame. Real shame. Personal shame. Not something out of a book or sermon or prayer or tossed about in a therapy session. Face to face stark blazing shame. The type that leaves a knot in the pit of your stomach.

Later that night I had a reckoning while flipping through the pages of my battered worn down old copy of 'Bernadette and Lourdes' by Michel de Saint-Pierre. The beast was upon me.

> "Then lowering her voice, Bernadette told of strange things. 'Whilst I was praying I heard shouting, confused voices that challenged each other and clashed together. It was like a thousand angry people shouting. It was horrible. The loudest voice shouted, 'Save yourself! Save yourself!' Bernadette added that the Lady had raised her head and frowned, looking in the direction of the river.
> Then, 'the voices fled in all directions.'"[1]

1. Michele de Saint-Pierre, *Bernadette and Lourdes* (Garden City: Image Books, 1955), 34

THE REFUGE OF SINNERS

Was there ever a time in human history that Satan didn't apply his arts? No. His fall from grace is from the beginning. He was with us in the Garden and will be with us until the end of time.

I put the book down, and the bad voice was in my head. Don't read this, ignore this. It means nothing to you. Put it away. Push it away. Then my phone went off. It was her. A good night face and a heart were on the screen.

The voice was in her head as well. Reach out to him, reach out. Now, right now. Coincidences do happen, of this there is no doubt but a calculated manipulation can happen as well.

There are those who say that mankind is the master of manipulation. Mankind may have mastered the art of manipulation, but mankind is not the master of manipulation. For to believe that lie is to be manipulated. And I was being manipulated.

It was surreal and disturbing. It was like a spiritual game of Poker. The moment I doubted my card hand the Devil drew an Ace. It was that fast and that simple.

Any average spiritually blind dope would ignore the book and respond to her with a smile emoji and probably feel very good about it. But I had peaked beneath the curtain and saw what was behind it. I could not claim to be just a spiritual ignoramus who actually thought two plus two equals four and the Devil was only a movie prop. In the realm of the demons, two plus two never equals four and the Devil is the head guy.

I put the phone on silence, flipped it over and laid it down on the nightstand. I kept reading the book.

> "The ecstasy came to an end, and the crowds surrounded Bernadette. 'Well what did she say to you?' 'The Lady's eyes left me for a moment,' the child replied, 'and looked into the distance above my head. When she looked at me again I asked what had made her so sad and she said simply,
> 'Pray for sinners!'"[2]

2. Michele de Saint-Pierre, *Bernadette and Lourdes*, 44

Pray for sinners. Ah, the simplest request that gets the least attention. Pray for us sinners, oh you true refuge of sinners.

When the book finally made it back into the nightstand, the words of my daughter came back again. "I'm proud of you, dad."

Pride. A word, from the spiritual viewpoint, that can have two meanings, one good and one bad. Which definition fit me? Both, neither? The buzz sound of my phone stopped my coursing pondering. I knew it was another text from her. The devil wasn't going to give up; he could sense my nagging remorse and he was pushing her. I ignored it again. It went off again and again, I ignored it.

"You're not gonna get me back in that way, I know what you're doing, you son of a bitch," I said firmly into the air. "I know it's you, you bastard. You can kiss my ass," I said even stronger and with a pinch of anger. I was being played and I knew it and that angered him. "Now I'm mad, you . . . you and your freaking games, you have two people so tangled up, you no good bastard."

Anger can be dangerous, it can lead you to the dark side, to steal a phrase from Yoda, but it can also be a powerful friend.

Anger can give you single-mindedness at times when pointed in the right direction and I was angry. Angry that I allowed my free will to be driven by passions; angry that I was prideful and self-centered rather than think about my family first; angry because things were already screwed up enough without a third party demon fanning the flames of a text.

But in the end it all came back to me, all of it. She wouldn't be texting me if I had not made that first move. My daughter would be justified in her affections if I had not put my own lust ahead of her trust. And the demons would be off tormenting some other poor sucker if I didn't' hand them the tool to beat my brains out.

I needed a refuge; I needed a sanctuary from the world, somewhere to hide and quite my mind to give me time to sort things out. And I knew exactly where I needed to go.

✳

Bernadette was 14 years old when she had her visions. She described the beautiful 'Lady' to be a girl between 16 and 17 years old, barely 2 years older than Bernadette and hardly a 'lady', at least in terms of her age. But Bernadette was a peasant who knew only extreme poverty, the most abject misery and to Bernadette, the ladyship of Mary was perceived by her overall glorified appearance and not by her apparent age. Mary appeared regal and yet, not beyond Bernadette's station in life. This poor ignorant child was lifted up and transformed. And in her lifetime she never became wealthy; she never became contented and suffered both physically and mentally. As Mary had promised, earthly happiness would elude her. But she was transformed, because she knew the truth. And ultimately, where her true destiny belonged.

XIII

SECOND CONFESSION

I WAS STIFF NECKED, like our ancestors. Weak. Willful. Obstinate. Sinful. Unrepentant. John the Baptist fired off his warning, "Repent for the kingdom of heaven is at hand."[4] Was it? Did it come? Is it still here? Looking at the world today one could argue the answer to all those questions is, undoubtedly no. But what is in plain sight and what is only hidden by our own pig-headed selfishness.

I had the kingdom of heaven shoved right in my face and still I rejected it. Like Peter, like all the others, they ran. But they redeemed themselves mightily. They cast aside their blinders and saw God face to face on the shore of a lake. Could I make that same leap of faith?

That was doubtful. Falling short of the mark became easier and more fun. The sex was too good, way too good. The intimate personal relationship was deep and long, evolving over many years. The conversations and small talk was enjoyable. It was all about me and what I wanted and needed.

Being a man, in the masculine sense of the word, was always an excuse to do whatever I wanted as a cheater. My carnal essentials were beyond my power to control to my twisted way of thinking. I was a victim of nature. The capacity to choose right from wrong was totally diminished by DNA strands passed down from some hairy caveman 500 generations ago. It was his fault; his need to survive that drove me to frequent crappy motel rooms and dark parking lots. Always point the finger backwards if you want to find the basic reason for doing anything. Just don't point the finger at yourself and you'll be fine.

I met my lady later that afternoon for a high tea of sorts. Coffee and sex. But I left feeling very unsettled, almost sick to my stomach. I literally felt sick, queasy. What was I doing? This is what it must feel like to be addicted to drugs or alcohol.

You fight it, give in, get the high and then get despondent over your inability to cope. But the real addict gets over that feel sorry phase quickly and is back on the high horse, or naked woman in my case.

So what is solution, what does the addict do when they finally hit bottom and begin their journey back to the light? They ask their higher power for help. They give it to God. They admit their shortcomings. They seek support. All very simple steps. Admit you're in the dregs of the wine barrel and then be determined to climb out. Was I ready to give it up?

My daughter was the push. This last covert get together, as satisfying as the sex was, did nothing but convince me I was in the basement room with the dregs, the squeezing's poured out on a dirty floor. Trying to come up with a way out was much more difficult than I expected. It wasn't just the sex. I tried to tell myself many times that sex was the only reason I was even involved at all and I could walk away anytime that I got bored with her, but that wasn't the truth. I was invested in this relationship with so many shared experiences, happy and sad, so many long conversations and confessions of our deepest uncertainties. Revelations of our most closely held secrets. In reality, I would be giving up on my best friend.

A course of action needed to be applied. Ignoring texts or calls would only take me so far out of the barrel before I answered the phone. Desire and the devil would make sure that I answered. Thoughts and ideas came and went. Finally, I decided to take a ride.

The basilica was closed but the large rectory lights were on. It was only around seven PM and usually something would be happening but there was no activity around the church other than a few people walking about the grounds praying along the outdoor 'stations of the cross'. I wasn't even sure what door to knock on but I walked around until I found a door bell button. A few rings brought an older man with white hair to the door.

"Yes", he said through the glass storm door.

"Oh, hello, I'm sorry for ringing, but was trying to find the name of a priest that works here."

"Yes, what's his name?", he replied again.

"I don't know his name, but he's about five-ten, maybe in his late forties, early fifties. Light colored hair."

"What's your business with Father?" he asked, but not mentioning a name.

"I was just wondering if I could speak with him or if you could give him my number."

He handed a small tablet through the open door and I wrote down my name and number. I also put under it the words, the Saint Michaels Prayer, in parenthesis. He took it and closed the door.

Two days later and unknown number rang on up on my phone, an out of state area code. I almost didn't answer it since spam calls have been bouncing in from every possible area.

"Hello?"

"You asked me to call you. What's so important that you'd bother an old priest for my information," he said with a bit of off-hand humor, but clearly not mocking me.

"Yes hi, thanks for calling me. I was just wondering if I could come up and have a chat sometime, maybe finish our conversation."

"Well, unfortunately I won't be at the basilica anymore. I'm in New York State and I will be leaving for Rome next weekend.

"Oh," was my only response.

"I'm here now, so, talk," he said matter quite of fact.

I didn't know where to begin, so I started as they say, at the beginning. The whole sordid tale, the nasty parts and the pleasant parts as well. I told him about my daughters' words of praise and about Saint Bernadette's words of warning.

I told him about my experiences in the mystical world and how the Holy Spirit shoved words inside my brain while sitting at the basilica. We spoke about the devil playing his games and about my one night of demonic madness. We also spoke about loss. My loss, in what I was really giving up and how I didn't want to lose her but also about what I would gain in return. Give up a bit of happiness and a whole lot of pleasure and gain back my pride . . . and my soul.

That weekend I went back to confession at the basilica. I saw the old man who answered the door at the rectory and realized he was a priest. I stood in line at the room he entered and then went in when my turn came. Explanations and a short synopsis were in order. He remembered me asking for the information about his colleague and was glad we spoke. There was no need to go into the long and detailed accounting of the situation. His requirements were clear and simple and my answers needed to be the same.

Later that night, my phone went off. A text of a heart. Tomorrow would be a better time to clear the deck, but at that moment, it was time for the prayer of protection.

The days that followed were full of tears. I had no idea how much losing her would affect me personally, the devil be damned. This was real loss, I felt crushed, more than I could even imagine. Any self-protecting ideas for this being primarily a sexual liaison were dashed. She was so important to me that I started to falter. But I knew what I had to do, even if I didn't want to do it; the key for the addict, knowing and then doing.

Meeting over coffee and running through each scenario left her saddened. I could see she was struggling since for her, our relationship meant real love and affection, something that was otherwise absent in her life. Yet understanding came to her naturally and this dilemma could never be rectified.

We both left the coffee shop broken in pieces. If I could be with her I would, I wanted to be more now than ever. She said her life would never be the same without me in it. But that was not possible. What was possible was to acknowledge that fact and try to move along with my life.

The release I felt was overwhelming. It was as though a great heavy shroud was pulled from my shoulders. All the guilt melted away and I was new again. The devil surely was not happy and was most likely carefully placing another stone in my path that I might stumble upon, but it wouldn't be the old stone.

The old stone was picked up and tossed back into the abyss from whence it came.

Holy Mary, mother of God, pray for us sinners, for me and for the many.

✳

Once in a great notion the truth becomes a reality. God's own creation is capable of the most wondrous of things as well as the most debased acts. Humans are very good at hiding from the truth even when it is jammed inside a skull full of avoidance.

Truth became reality when Jesus became one of us. God was no longer outside of our world but was now fully a part of it. People spoke with God, ate with God. But to live a life of avoidance is to live outside of that truth.

And the truth hurts sometimes. And it hurt me, very much. And it still does. For not a day goes by that I don't wish a different outcome could have been possible.

There has never been a woman as kind, gentle, generous, caring, loving or as approachable as her, never. She was everything. What I lost was the most perfect companion.

But truth is truth . . . and the truth is I didn't lose her. She was never mine to lose.

She belonged to another man. And she still does.

End

www.ingramcontent.com/pod-product-compliance
Lightning Source LLC
LaVergne TN
LVHW021612080426
835510LV00019B/2537